How to Use an Airbrush

ROBERT DOWNIE

KALMBACH
BOOKS

Printed in the United States of America

06 07 08 09   10 9 8 7 6 5 4

Visit our website at http://kalmbachbooks.com
Secure online ordering available

Publisher's Cataloging-in-Publication
Provided by Quality Books, Inc.

Downie, Robert, 1960-
    How to use an airbrush /
Robert Downie. — 1st ed.
p. cm.
ISBN: 0-89024-287-9

    1. Models and modelmaking.
2. Airbrush art. 3. Spray painting.
I. Title.

TT154.D69 2001   745.59'28
              QBI01-200133

Art director: Kristi Ludwig
Book design: Sabine Beaupré

All photos by Robert Downie except where noted

Contents

Introduction

One of the greatest challenges a modeler faces is creating a great finish on a model. An airbrush is a tool that can help immensely. But while some modelers have mastered the use of this tool, others simply lack the experience—or confidence—to achieve the desired results. In fact, too many of you already own an airbrush, but are afraid of it. You find it easier to leave it in the box, and instead continue to use "spray bombs"—paint from aerosol cans.

The airbrush unjustly intimidates too many people. This book will help you learn to use this wonderfully versatile tool. With a little practice and experimentation, you too can quickly master its use.

There are books and magazines that deal with airbrushing, but most cater to artists who paint flat, two-dimensional surfaces: T-shirts, posters, and canvas. This book is written specifically for modelers. You want detailed instruction on how to use your airbrush to paint three-dimensional surfaces, replicating a variety of realistic finishes on your favorite models. The book will teach you to achieve many surface finishes with an airbrush. And I'll give you information about the mechanics of layering the airbrushed finish with other techniques.

This book will help you in three ways: (1) It will give you background on the equipment—the types of airbrushes you can use for various purposes. (2) It will introduce you to methods of applying appropriate paints. (3) It will provide a wealth of additional tips, techniques, and detailed step-by-step instructions to help you achieve a dazzling array of finishes.

Each chapter will cover a project. Each will teach you how to achieve various finishes on particular types of models, showing you the materials and tools you will need. Also, I'll show you some of the problems and specific effects associated with the improper use of materials.

As in many areas of modeling, the more practice you get, the better model builder you will become. Most of the techniques shown in this book I've used successfully for many years. However, a few of the techniques I tried out myself for the first time, just to demonstrate some additional options for these projects.

I suggest you use the same combination: practice to master common skills, and experiment to learn new ones. With the proper tools and experience, and a little trial and error, anyone can learn to use his or her airbrush with a minimum of stress and effort.

Believe me, once you achieve that first truly great finish, you will understand the immense feeling of accomplishment. You will be well on your way to mastering a tool that has revolutionized how paint finishes are applied to models. Success breeds confidence. Soon, you will be confident enough to tackle any paint finish you desire on your models.

I would like to thank all who helped guide me along the path towards completion of this book. First, I want to thank Pat Covert, whose friendship and encouragement means a lot to me. He was also the one who put me in touch with Kalmbach Books and the opportunity to write this book. Also, many thanks go to a college professor of mine, Joe Ferrer, a great teacher of professional modelmaking and painting. From him I learned most of the skills that I use both professionally and in my hobby. Finally, I want to thank my good friend Bob Holfels, an accomplished modelmaker skilled in the construction of many types of models. He generously allowed me to borrow a number of his models to study and photograph in preparing this book, and he answered my myriad questions on applying various new finishes. You will see a number of his models as examples throughout this book. I am forever indebted to him for the help he has not only given to me but shared with you as well.

Getting Started: Equipment, Materials, and Basic Techniques

This chapter will introduce you to the basic tools, materials, and techniques needed to use an airbrush properly. I will show you various types of airbrushes, some of the effects you can achieve with them, and some options in choosing air-propellant systems.

Why use an airbrush? What makes it so superior to a spray can? For one thing, an airbrush gives far greater control over the volume and pressure of the air flow. It also gives you greater control of the consistency (and the color) of the paint that is being sprayed.

In contrast, a spray can gives you lots of paint delivered under lots of pressure. The volume of paint and the air pressure are fixed; you can't adjust them. Too much paint flows out at once, obliterating detail. It also causes paint to run or creates thin spots on sharp edges or raised details.

Or the spray-can paint flows out under too little pressure, causing a thick, grainy, "orange-peel" effect.

While it is not impossible to achieve a good finish with spray cans, it is far easier to achieve a great finish with an airbrush.

Fig. 1-1. The most basic Testors airbrush setup, available in discount stores for under $30. It includes almost everything you will need to spray, except for paint and thinner.

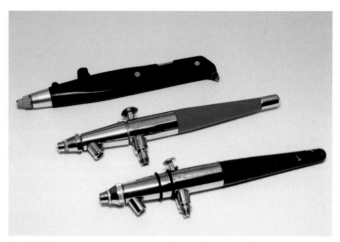

Fig. 1-2. Here are three common internal-mix airbrushes: a Testors/Aztek Model Master brush, a Paasche VL, and a Badger Crescendo. All three provide good performance and control, and parts are readily obtainable.

How does an airbrush work? The compressed-air source forces air over a paint nozzle (inside the airbrush). This creates a vacuum that pulls paint up into the airflow from a paint container—an attached jar or cup. When the paint hits the air stream, it is broken up into a mist of small particles that are shot out of the working end of the tool.

The basic setup

The basic equipment needed for an airbrush outfit includes an airbrush, an air source, paint, thinner, plenty of mixing jars, paper towels and rags, stirring sticks, and a safe, well-lit place to paint. You need not spend a lot of money to purchase an expensive airbrush or extra equipment. You can pick up a basic Testors single-action, external-mix setup with propellant (see fig. 1-1) for under $30. Even with this simplest setup, with a little practice you can achieve finishes far superior to any you would get by using a spray can. This inexpensive tool offers a good chance to teach yourself some techniques and finish several models before making a commitment to move up to a more expensive airbrush and compressor.

Basically, this airbrush works like a lot like a spray can: when you press the trigger, paint flows onto the model (see fig. 1-3, upper half). However, you control the paint flow in two ways: by mixing the paint to the proper consistency and by controlling the amount of air forced through the airbrush. And you can custom-mix your paint and thinner to any color you desire.

A step up from the basic airbrush is the single-action, internal-mix airbrush. This type of airbrush delivers a finer spray pattern than the basic external-mix airbrush and is available with a variety of nozzles ranging from fine to high-flow. However, the amount of paint delivered is fixed.

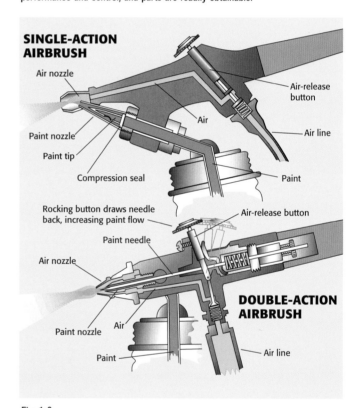

SINGLE-ACTION AIRBRUSH

Air nozzle

Air-release button

Air

Paint nozzle

Air line

Paint tip

Compression seal

Paint

Rocking button draws needle back, increasing paint flow

Air-release button

Paint needle

Air nozzle

Air

Paint nozzle

DOUBLE-ACTION AIRBRUSH

Paint

Air line

Fig. 1-3

The dual-action airbrush

The best all-around airbrush for many modelers is what is known as a dual-action airbrush (see fig. 1-3, lower half). The button you push with your finger controls both pressure and paint flow at the same time. Pushing down on the trigger controls the airflow. Push down a little, and a small volume of air is precisely delivered. Push down a lot, and more air is delivered. Pull back on the trigger slowly, and the paint flow gradually

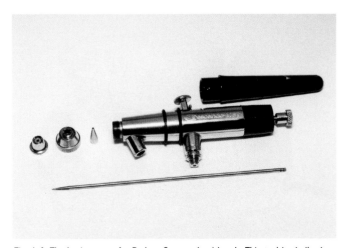

Fig. 1-4. The basic parts of a Badger Crescendo airbrush. This tool is similar in parts and design to other internal-mix airbrushes.

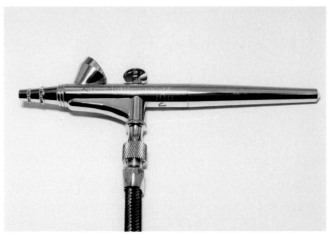

Fig. 1-5. The Rich Model AB 200 airbrush is an excellent choice if you want to achieve superb fine-line details. Many seasoned modelers own several airbrushes to achieve different results.

changes from a fine mist to a heavy flow. With a bit of practice—and the proper consistency of paint—you will be able to control the paint and airflow with precision to achieve anything from a slight pebble-grained or stippled finish to a smooth, heavy, glossy finish.

Most dual-action airbrushes have optional nozzles and needles, used to create different effects. Generally, fine, medium, and high-flow nozzles are available for most airbrushes.

Most of the airbrush work I do is with this type of airbrush. A couple of the most common dual-action, internal-mix airbrushes are the Paasche VL and Badger 175 Crescendo. Having used both of these airbrushes extensively, I feel either will work well for most modelers. I like them both. The Crescendo works especially well for high-flow, gloss paint jobs on model car exterior finishes.

Testors Model Master and Aztek lines are also good airbrushes. They are especially easy to clean and maintain, and parts and accessories are commonly available at most hobby shops.

You can see some of these airbrushes in fig. 1-2: the Model Master airbrush on top, the Paasche VL in the middle, and the Badger 175 Crescendo on the bottom. Before you purchase one, I suggest that you check with local retailers on the availability of common repair parts such as replacement tips and needles. Since you can get great results with different brands, why not consider buying one for which you can easily get replacement parts locally?

Also, ask friends who already own airbrushes to recommend their favorite choice. If you are lucky, they may let you try out their airbrush for a test run.

If you already own an airbrush, don't worry. With practice, you should be able to achieve professional results. And if you follow good care and maintenance, you shouldn't need replace-

ment parts too often. With any airbrush, keep all manuals that come with it for parts reference and assembly instructions. Often, replacement parts and accessories are available directly from the manufacturer.

Figure 1-4 shows the basic components of the Badger Crescendo airbrush, partially disassembled. This type of assembly is common to both the Badger and Paasche. These are the parts you will typically deal with when cleaning your airbrush. At left, you see the basic nozzle, and next to the nozzle is the airbrush head. Next is the "seat," the conical piece (trapped between the head and the airbrush body) that controls the paint flow over the needle. Next to the seat is the airbrush itself. Above it is the rear cover, which slides on and off the rear of the airbrush to access the air control and needle-locking mechanisms. Underneath the airbrush is the needle.

The basic assembly is easy to memorize. Read your owner's manual carefully for assembly and cleaning instructions for your specific brand. Once familiar with it, you can quickly clean your airbrush or install different needles, nozzles, or replacement components.

Specialty airbrushes

Specialty airbrushes are available to help you achieve even finer, more detailed results. A fine-line airbrush can be used for intricate camouflage and other detailing techniques that even the "fine" nozzles on a general-purpose airbrush cannot achieve. Figure 1-5 shows a Rich Model AB 200 airbrush made specifically for fine-line detail. This airbrush is used in several projects later in this book. This type of nozzle allows you to use your airbrush as a writing or drawing instrument, and delivers the paint precisely—down to a fine line.

Fig. 1-6. Carbon dioxide (CO_2) tanks like this one provide a quiet source of pressure but must be refilled periodically. Kalmbach photo

Fig. 1-7. This Sears compressor is an example of many that are available on the market from varied sources. Like all hobby compressors, it is an oil-less design, providing a stream of clean air to propel the paint.

Fixed-supply air sources

To propel the paint through your airbrush, you need an air source. Testors makes cans of compressed air called Propel, which work well. If you only occasionally use an airbrush, this may be an economical solution. You can also purchase a special tank at a hardware or automotive store which holds compressed air that you can use as a propellant. The downside to these approaches is that you may run out of pressure midway through a project. You must stop your work to go out and buy a refill.

Another propellant source is a tank of CO_2—carbon dioxide (see fig. 1-6). These tanks can be purchased through welding supply houses, and they will give you a quiet, moisture-free source of compressed propellant for your paint. Beware of the inherent dangers of compressed air tanks. The tanks are heavy, and once empty, must be refilled. But I have heard of modelers who used this type of propellant and were quite satisfied with the setup.

Electric compressors

The most favored source of compressed air for modelers is an electric compressor. Numerous types and models are available, many made specifically for modelers. As long as the compressor is an oil-less style, it should be suitable for model use. Many larger shop-style compressors have air tanks; the compressor runs for a while to fill the tank, then while you are operating your airbrush it is quiet. The downside to large compressors (and many small ones) is the noise they generate. They can be quite loud. If you are considering purchasing one, make sure that its use does not create too much of a racket for your family or neighbors to endure!

Most modelers can use a common, small compressor (see fig. 1-7). This type of hobby compressor generates plenty of airflow for an airbrush, and can be used with or without a pressure reg-

ulator or moisture trap. I have found that the airflow from this type of compressor works well most of the time.

The most common problem you may encounter is a buildup of moisture after extended use; this results in moisture being sprayed onto the model while you are painting. You can usually hear the moisture whistling through the air hose just before it travels through the airbrush. If not, you will see and hear it spit onto the surface you are painting. At this point, you should set the model aside to dry thoroughly, then check the finish to see if it must be sanded and recoated with paint. Often, the grainy pattern caused by the moisture evaporates, and the surface finish is only mildly affected. A quick scuffing with a polishing cloth or fine-grit sandpaper will correct the problem.

If this moisture spraying occurs, disconnect the air hose from the airbrush and allow the compressor to run for a few minutes. This will dry out the hose.

To avoid the problem of moisture damaging the finish of your model in the first place, you can use an inline moisture trap or one attached directly to the compressor (see fig. 1-8). This filter can generally be purchased where airbrush supplies are sold, or

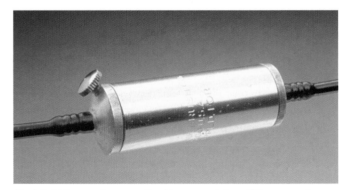

Fig. 1-8. Adding a moisture trap like this to your air line will keep water from ruining your paint job. Kalmbach photo

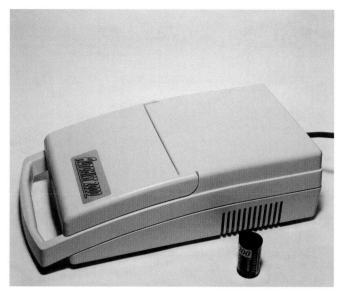

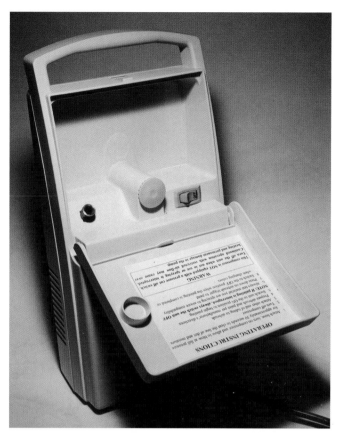

Figs. 1-9 and 1-10. The Auto Mist compressor is a great new compressor, designed for hobbyists and medical uses. It is relatively low in cost, and provides quiet operation with almost no moisture buildup in the air hoses.

at a larger hardware retailer that deals with large, professional-grade air compressors.

Low-noise compressors

Because both noise and moisture buildup had been a nuisance with my previous airbrushing outfit, I purchased a compressor made specifically for low-noise output and with an internal moisture trap. Several manufacturers make compressors with these features for airbrush artists, but their cost can be high. You can compare the price tags of such units at larger art supply stores.

Alternatively, you can look for a compressor made by Auto Mist (see figs. 1-9 and 1-10) that was actually developed for the medical industry. It even meets FDA requirements! It proved also to be a great compressor for hobbyists, and it is now marketed to them as well. The cost is competitive with other hobby compressors.

So if noise is a big concern, you may want to find one of these. It is extremely quiet, and unless you use it for hours at a time, moisture buildup is not a problem. It is currently available with an optional pressure regulator, and future models may feature an internal regulator as standard equipment. The compressor is light and portable, and it can be operated flat on a horizontal surface, upright, or mounted to a wall.

Paint thinners

Whatever type of paint you will be spraying through your airbrush, you will need the proper thinner to thin the paint and to clean the airbrush after each use. You need to have the proper type of thinner for the paint you are using (see fig. 1-11). Most brands of paint have their own thinners/reducers, specifically formulated for their particular paint. This is the thinner you should start and practice with. Once you have become familiar with a paint-thinner combination, you may want to experiment

Fig. 1-11. A selection of common paint thinners for paints used by modelers.

with some techniques that use alternative thinners (discussed later in this book).

In general, most hobby enamels can be thinned either with their "house" brand thinner, or with general-purpose lacquer thinners, which are available in most discount stores. These general-use thinners work well to mix with hobby enamels and to clean the airbrush after use. However, they do not mix well with automotive lacquers, which require their own brand-specific thinner/reducers for proper thinning.

Many hobby acrylic paints can be thinned with common reducers such as distilled water, denatured alcohol, rubbing alcohol, or even window cleaner. Once you have tried a manufacturer's brand-name acrylic thinner, you may want to experiment with other "household" thinners to see if one works with

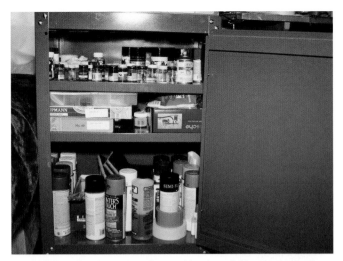

Fig. 1-12. Hazardous fumes are a danger with paint and thinners, so store them in a fireproof, enclosed storage area. A side benefit is that a cabinet like this can be locked to keep the materials away from small children.

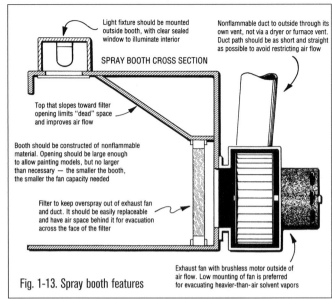

SPRAY BOOTH CROSS SECTION

Light fixture should be mounted outside booth, with clear sealed window to illuminate interior

Nonflammable duct to outside through its own vent, not via a dryer or furnace vent. Duct path should be as short and straight as possible to avoid restricting air flow

Top that slopes toward filter opening limits "dead" space and improves air flow

Booth should be constructed of nonflammable material. Opening should be large enough to allow painting models, but no larger than necessary — the smaller the booth, the smaller the fan capacity needed

Filter to keep overspray out of exhaust fan and duct. It should be easily replaceable and have air space behind it for evacuation across the face of the filter

Exhaust fan with brushless motor outside of air flow. Low mounting of fan is preferred for evacuating heavier-than-air solvent vapors

Fig. 1-13. Spray booth features

Fig. 1-14. This is a low-cost paint booth, constructed from a large cardboard box, using a filter to pull the paint and fumes out of the booth.

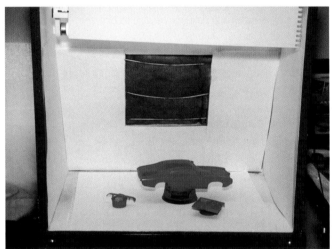

Fig. 1-15. Here is a homemade spray booth, designed to provide a large, bright area in which to paint. Features include good lighting and a flameproof fan assembly to pull filtered air and fumes out of the booth.

your brand of acrylic. (Sometimes these thinners do not mix well with the paint but offer an economical way to clean the airbrush afterwards.)

Experimentation will yield a variety of results. Once you achieve good results, remember the process for further use! Take notes for your personal reference. However, in general, the most reliable results occur with thinners made by paint manufacturers for their specific brands and types of paint. It is always wise to have the recommended thinner on hand before you experiment with alternative thinners.

Storage

You want to carefully store your paints and thinners in an enclosed area. Many can emit harmful fumes, and they can be fire hazards. A secure metal enclosure is the best protection from fire and vapor hazards (see fig. 1-12). Keep it locked, so the contents are inaccessible to small inquisitive children. Also, always have a fire extinguisher handy in your work area.

Lighting and ventilation

If you paint in an enclosed area, you will need to make or purchase a spray booth suitable for your models. Several manufacturers make such booths. Standard features should include a built-in fan, filters, and a hose to remove the fumes (see fig. 1-13).

You can make your own low-cost enclosure from a large box, and use standard furnace/air conditioning filters available in hardware stores (see fig. 1-14). You will want to paint with good lighting. A small fluorescent light fixture mounted to the top of the spray booth is a good solution.

To remove the paint vapors and overspray, a flameproof fan is necessary. These fans can be ordered from standard home and industrial supply houses and use a flexible metal hose to remove the vapors. An example of this type of homemade spray booth is seen in fig. 1-15. This setup is at a comfortable height for painting, is bright and well lit, and a fan and hose in the back efficiently exhaust filtered fumes from the work area.

Fig. 1-16. This is a common painter's respirator, which you'll need whenever painting with any toxic spray paints or thinners. When properly worn, you should not be able to smell any paint vapors.

Respirators

Figure 1-16 shows a common type of paint respirator. You should wear one of these whenever spraying any lacquer, enamel, or acrylic paints not labeled as nontoxic by their manufacturers. If there is any doubt—unless the paint and thinner you are using are both specifically labeled as nontoxic—wear the respirator. It can be purchased at automotive paint and body-shop supply stores and is well worth the investment. You should not smell any paint or thinner odors while wearing the mask if it's properly fit.

If you love to build and paint models, and want to continue to do so for years to come, wear one of these respirators to prevent damage to your lungs from breathing harmful vapors.

If you are sensitive to paint vapors or wish not to wear a respirator, there are several brands of acrylic paints that are non-toxic. These paints may not spray as smoothly as enamel or lacquer-based paints, but their relative lack of odor and toxicity is definitely a plus for people, especially those sensitive or

Safety with Solvents

Organic (carbon-based) solvents found in paints and thinners can do serious harm if you inhale them or absorb them through the skin. Here's a partial list of the solvents found in some model paints and thinners:

Product	Solvents included
Accu-paint thinner	acetone, methyl ethyl ketone
Floquil Dio-Sol, airbrush thinner	naphtha, toluene, xylene
Scalecoat and Scalecoat II thinner	naphtha, xylene
Clear coats and other lacquers	acetone, toluene, xylene
Common lacquer thinner	methyl ethyl ketone, methyl isobutyl ketone, toluene

Short-term effects of high-level exposure to these solvents include breathing difficulty, dizziness, fatigue, nausea, and headaches. Severe cases can result in loss of consciousness and respiratory failure. Obviously, if you experience any of the initial symptoms, get into fresh air immediately and take steps to see that the exposure isn't repeated. Seek medical attention promptly if any symptoms persist.

Long-term effects of contact with dangerous levels of the solvents can include deterioration of bone marrow, blood disorders, and nervous system damage.

These products can be used safely. By providing adequate ventilation (a spray booth) and wearing an approved respirator, such as the one in fig. 1-16, you can keep exposure to these chemicals well within safe levels. Look for a chemical-cartridge respirator that fits your face properly and doesn't allow any air in except through the filters. The masks are available in several styles and sizes. Follow the manufacturer's direction regarding proper fitting and maintenance.

Safety labels of paints and thinners usually list the type of chemical cartridge needed to protect you from that product's ingredients. For most of the solvents listed above, a TC-23C cartridge (or equivalent) approved by NIOSH and MSHA is recommended. This number can be found on the cartridge itself as well as on the packaging for the mask and cartridge.

Eye protection is also a must when working with solvents. A stray splash or spray of solvent can easily injure your eyes, so a pair of safety goggles should be standard equipment.

This information isn't designed to scare you away from the solvent-based paints. However, it's important to understand the need for safety and the methods you should take to protect yourself and your family.

Solvent disposal

Never dispose of your old thinner or paint by pouring it down a drain. Also refrain from sneaking out to the back yard and dumping it behind the garage.

Use an old solvent can (never a glass container) to collect old paint and solvents. Many local municipalities have special collection dates for hazardous materials once or twice a year. Others require these materials to be dropped off at a central location.

– from *Painting and Weathering Railroad Models,* by Jeff Wilson (Kalmbach Books)

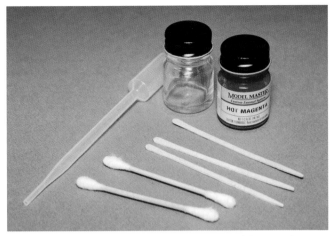

Fig. 1-17. Handy items for mixing and transferring paint and thinner, and to clean up jars and lids.

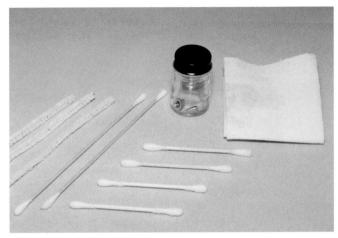

Fig. 1-18. Some basic supplies to clean your airbrush.

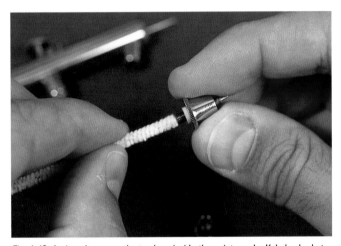

Fig. 1-19. A pipe cleaner works to clean inside the paint nozzle. Kalmbach photo

Fig. 1-20. Flushing your airbrush with fresh thinner after every painting session will make it easier to tear it down and clean it. Kalmbach photo

allergic to the odors. Also, sometimes you may wish to paint your models in a setting where odors may be a nuisance to others, such as in an apartment complex with many other people living nearby. Use common sense and care when choosing both your paints and breathing apparatus.

Mixing paint

To mix your paint, a number of simple items (see fig. 1-17) will make the job easier. Plastic pipettes are handy for measuring precise amounts of paint and thinners into common airbrush jars. They allow you to transfer the liquid without spilling and make it much easier to add a few drops of thinner, especially if you are using a large container of lacquer thinner. Testors sells these pipettes individually, and they are also available pre-packaged along with ½-ounce paint mixing jars.

Small, flat wooden sticks are great for stirring paint, either in the original jar or in the airbrush jar after adding the thinner. These sticks can be found in art supply or craft stores. Cotton swabs made with wooden sticks will also come in handy to clean the airbrush and paint jar lids. They also make great paint stirrers, if you break off one end of the swab. These swabs are available at most grocery stores.

Cleaning

You need basic supplies on hand to clean your airbrush and paint jars (see fig. 1-18). Common pipe cleaners work well to clean the airbrush itself and the inlet hoses. Soak the pipe cleaner in a solvent such as lacquer thinner or rubbing alcohol, depending on the type of paint you used, and guide it through the parts to clean out the paint residue (see fig. 1-19). Then run a dry pipe cleaner through the parts. To finish the job, run some clear thinner through the airbrush to make sure it is thoroughly clean (fig. 1-20).

Cotton swabs are handy to clean the airbrush body and head assemblies, and to get into tight areas (fig. 1-21). These swabs are available in different sizes; most are available in grocery stores. The longer ones can be found in electronics hardware stores, where they are used to clean electronic equipment.

Don't forget to keep a roll of paper towels handy, to clean up any accidental spills and the airbrush body and paint jars. And empty paint jars are useful to clean airbrush heads; just fill the jar with thinner and drop the heads in to soak (fig. 1-22).

Testing spray patterns

Once you have assembled your airbrush, air source, paint, cleaning supplies, and respirator, and created a suitable place to

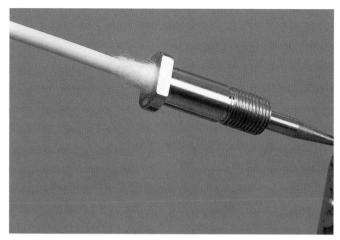

Fig. 1-21. Using a cotton swab dipped in thinner is a good way to clean the inside of the paint tip. Kalmbach photo

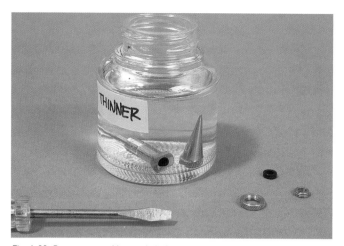

Fig. 1-22. Remove any rubber seals before soaking airbrush parts in thinner or other cleaning solvents. Kalmbach photo

BADGER 175 CRESCENDO MEDIUM TIP

BADGER 175 CRESCENDO HIGH-FLOW TIP

BADGER 175 CRESCENDO FINE TIP

RICH AB-200 FINELINE

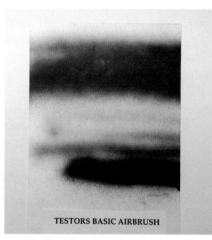

TESTORS BASIC AIRBRUSH

Figs. 1-23 to 1-27. Typical paint effects, line weights, and spray patterns for various airbrushes and their tips and needles.

paint, you are ready to teach yourself how all these elements work together. Start with scrap model bodies or sheets of plastic or cardboard. Practice mixing paints and thinners and test spraying them through the airbrush. If you have multiple nozzles, try each one to become familiar with the paint flow and the finish you can achieve with each particular nozzle. Use some of the actual paints you will be spraying onto your models.

Before using your airbrush on a model, test the spray patterns on some scrap material. Each airbrush has its own particular spraying characteristics, depending upon the paint you are using, the source of compressed air, and the distance you hold the airbrush from the surface.

You can see the differences in spray patterns of three different airbrushes using the same type of paint. Each test was set to spray the finest pattern with the airbrush held close to the card, ending with a progressively heavier application at the bottom.

As you can see in figs. 1-23 to 1-27, a wide variety of spray widths and precision were the result. Making your own reference chart like this—using your own airbrushes—is a good idea. It will help you choose the right tool for each job.

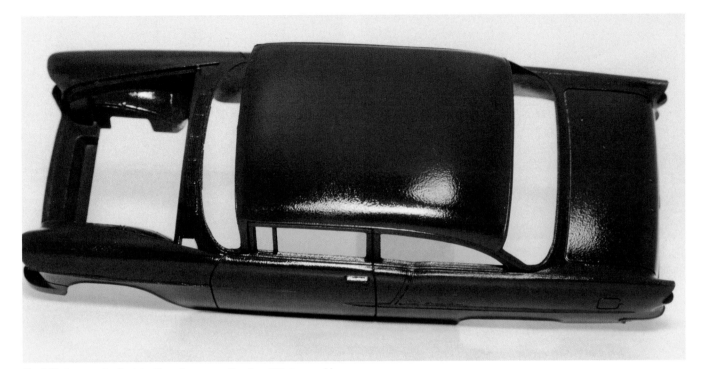

Fig. 1-28. An example of paint with an "orange-peel" surface. This is caused by not mixing enough thinner with the paint, or by using an inadequate airflow to propel the paint through the airbrush.

Cleaning your airbrush

To clean the airbrush after painting, disassemble the unit and clean all of the parts that paint has been in contact with. This may seem complicated at first, but after going through the disassembly-cleaning-reassembly sequence a few times, you will easily memorize the sequence, which does not take long to accomplish. Refer back to fig. 1-4 to see how simple most basic airbrush assemblies are.

Be diligent and keep your airbrush clean. Most problems occur from improper or incomplete cleaning and maintenance of the airbrush's components. Even tiny amounts of dried paint left inside the airbrush will disrupt the flow and pattern of the delivered air and paint mixture. Clean the parts thoroughly after each use for smooth, reliable operation.

If you have cleaned your airbrush and your paint mixture is correct, but the paint or thinner does not flow through it, or it sprays erratically, thoroughly clean the parts again. Keep a supply of paper towels, old rags, cotton swabs, and pipe cleaners handy—these are inexpensive, valuable tools to keep your airbrush clean and functioning well.

Troubleshooting

When painting your models, you may encounter various problems with paint finishes, whether you're using an airbrush or a spray can. Plan ahead, and you can minimize these potential problems. Some of the most common problems are easily solved. Too often, modelers will give up after experiencing just one small glitch, or end up stripping the paint to start over when that is not necessary.

"Orange-peel" finishes

One common problem appears as a thick, grainy paint surface, sometimes looking like sandpaper or "orange peel" (see fig. 1-28). This is caused primarily either by an improper paint mixture or by a lack of adequate air pressure. First, make sure your paint is thinned properly. For most applications, the proper consistency of paint to thinner is similar to the consistency of milk. When you mix your paint with the thinner and stir it, the result should generally have this milky consistency.

If the paint is settling onto the surface of your model with a thick and grainy appearance, your paint may be too thick. Add more thinner to your mixture and try it again.

Also, experiment with the distance you hold the airbrush from the surface of the model. The closer you hold it, the wetter and heavier the paint will be. However, most beginners are a bit timid with an airbrush and hold it too far away from the surface being painted. This also can contribute to a rough finish.

If you want to avoid problems, practice! Try out both good techniques and poor techniques. You will gain the knowledge of what can happen—and how to avoid it and improve your own paint finishes and techniques.

"Fisheyes"

Another common problem you may encounter is the appearance of small, sometimes circular voids of paint which the paint will not cover. These are commonly known as "fisheyes" (see figs. 1-29 and 1-30). Once they appear, they are difficult if not impossible to correct without stripping the paint and starting over.

This condition happens when the model surface has not been cleaned properly. Even small amounts of silicone, oil, grease,

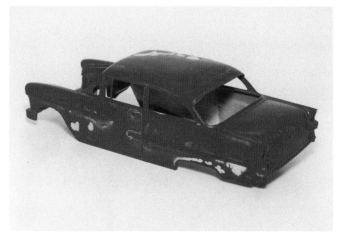

Figs. 1-29 and 1-30. Fisheyes (lack of paint adhesion) are caused by cleaning the surface of your model incompletely before painting.

Fig. 1-30. If you expect adhesion problems or are covering another coat that had fisheye problems, you can mix a product like Smoothie fisheye preventative into your paints.

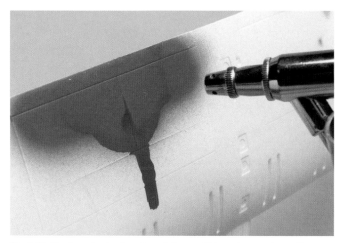

Fig. 1-31. Here's a classic view of a paint run—which you're sure to see if you don't keep your airbrush moving smoothly back and forth. Kalmbach photo

Fig. 1-32. A classic case of crazing and wrinkling of paint. This incompatibility occurs if you spray a lacquer over enamels—or over bare plastic—without first priming the plastic to accept lacquer-based paints.

fingerprints, or other dirt on the surface will cause this type of paint defect. If this happens, let the paint on your model dry, clean it thoroughly, and if the flaw is minor, sand the affected surface and try again. If this does not work and the problem recurs, you will need to strip the body and start over.

Some enamels and lacquers can be mixed with a fisheye preventative (see fig. 1-30). This type of product helps to avoid some problems in covering silicone or grease residue.

But the best course of action is to clean and dry your model thoroughly before you begin to paint it. Use warm, soapy water. Rinse it thoroughly with water, and dry it thoroughly. You can even use rubbing alcohol wiped over the plastic as an extra preventive measure, to remove any fingerprints you may have added to the surface as you prepared it to paint. Some window cleaners also work well to clean the model surface.

Runs and thin spots

Sometimes you might accidentally mix your paint with too much thinner. This makes it difficult for the paint to cover the model. It causes the paint to run and creates thin spots on high,

raised surfaces of the model. The solution is to adjust the paint consistency back to that of milk. Carefully add paint to the mixture, several drops at a time.

Avoid adding too much paint, creating the opposite effect: a grainy surface! If your paint does run (see fig. 1-31), let it dry thoroughly before you check to see whether it can be carefully sanded or if the body must be stripped.

Wrinkling

Wrinkling of a paint finish can occur when you overcoat one layer of paint with another. For one reason or another, the second coat is incompatible with the first. Sometimes the first coat has not dried thoroughly. Or the overcoat may be a different type of paint—a common occurrence if you try to spray a lacquer-based paint over enamel or bare plastic. Be sure to use the proper types of paint whenever adding layers of paint.

Figure 1-32 shows the effect of spraying lacquer over enamel. As you can see, the paint and plastic underneath has a rough, crazed texture; the surface of the body has been damaged by the lacquer thinner. Generally, you can spray almost any type of

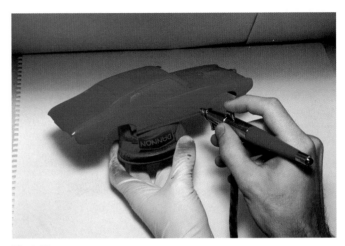

Figs. 1-33 to 1-35. This series of photos shows the proper painting stroke. Remember to start and finish beyond the surface of the model for the smoothest application of paint.

Fig. 1-34

Troubleshooting Tip

How can you fix a case of "overspray"—getting a splattering of paint off to the side while you're trying to paint a line?

• Have you cleaned the airbrush regularly?
• Is the tip of the needle bent? The best way to tell is to remove the needle from the airbrush and lightly drag it across your fingertip. Rotate the needle and do it again. You'll be able to feel a little "hook" to one side of the needle if it is bent. You can straighten it out by lightly dragging the tip over fine sandpaper until the hook is gone.
• Is the opening in the nozzle perfectly round or is it lopsided? Does it have a crack?
• Are you thinning the paint properly?
• Is this fresh paint? Old paint can separate and clump and clog the airbrush.

If you need replacement parts, contact your favorite supplier.

If you determine that your tip is bent (by gently drawing it across your finger), you might be able to fix it by lightly drawing the bent side along 600-grit sandpaper or a medium-grit sanding

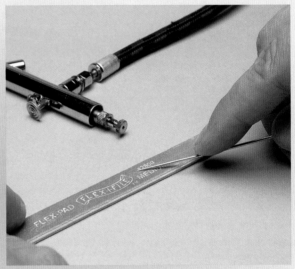

Fig. 1-37   Kalmbach photo

stick (see fig. 1-37). Just make one pass, then test the tip again on your finger. Test and repeat until the tip of the nozzle feels smooth. However, if the tip is cracked or severely bent, the only solution is to order a replacement needle.

Fig. 1-35

Fig. 1-36. Keep the airbrush perpendicular to the surface at all times, unless you are trying to create a special effect.

enamel or acrylic paint over lacquer, but you cannot spray lacquers over other types of paint.

The painting stroke

Figures 1-33 through 1-35 show the basic airbrush stroke. In fig. 1-33, you are just beginning to spray your paint. Figure 1-34 shows the middle of the stroke. Continue the painting stroke past the end of the model surface (fig. 1-35). Continuing the stroke beyond the end of the model ensures that a smooth, even amount of paint gets applied to the surfaces. This prevents color buildup and many paint thickness problems.

Figure 1-36 shows the airbrush held perpendicular to the surface of the model. Unless you are trying to achieve a special effect (discussed later in this book), always paint your models with the airbrush held perpendicular to the surface. This ensures a proper buildup of paint onto the model.

Notice that in the illustration I am wearing gloves and have attached the model to a cup for spraying. While painting, you always want to cover your hands. Disposable gloves are the best way to protect your hands from paint and solvents. And always create some form of paint stand to hold your models while you are painting. This way, your hands do not contact the parts being painted.

Once the parts are painted, you may want to use a dehydrator (see fig. 1-38), to help speed the drying process. Food dehydrators can be purchased in discount department stores, and are efficient at speeding up the drying process. They provide a warm, dry environment, with an upwards airflow that prevents dust from settling on the wet surfaces. The ideal temperature to dry the paint is between 95 to 100 degrees Fahrenheit. Be sure to check the temperature inside. If it gets above 115 degrees, leave the cover off and provide plenty of ventilation.

Fig. 1-38. A low-cost food dehydrator is a great companion for a modeler. It allows the paints to dry and cure on your models much quicker than in ambient air temperature and humidity.

You're ready!

At this point, you're ready to use your airbrush to paint some of your projects. In the following chapters, I'll lead you step by step through a number of projects, using different products and techniques to achieve a variety of airbrushed finishes.

Be creative! If you like a technique I've used on a particular project, don't feel constrained to use that technique only on that type of model. A technique used on a jet can be tried on a car. A technique used to bring a figure to life can be used on an airplane or a science fiction model. The techniques used throughout this book are very versatile; I encourage you to try them out on different types of models.

The main emphasis is to have fun trying new techniques—and to enjoy the sense of accomplishment you get when you have successfully achieved a desired finish on your model.

Let's have some fun and start painting!

2

The "Relic"

Simple Techniques Give Amazing Results on Vinyl or Resin Figures

Figure models are an ideal medium to showcase your talent with an airbrush. In general, a figure model allows you to be a bit "looser" with your painting style, both with your airbrush and with other paint details. For this project, I chose a vinyl figure, but the basic techniques can be used with figures in other mediums as well.

This figure is a Pro Modeler kit of Kathoga, the creature featured in the movie *The Relic*. One challenge in painting this model is that in the movie, you see very little color or detail on the creature. How does that affect the project?

Well, in my opinion, it allows for a lot more creativity. You may paint it in any color(s) you see fit.

In most cases, though, figure models feature colorful box art to use as a painting guide, as well as paint-color instructions in the assembly manual. This particular model has excellent box art to use as a guide. I kept the box top next to my spray booth as I did the fine detailing with the airbrush.

Besides box art or reference photos, you could use the colors and patterns of actual reptiles or amphibians to decorate your model. Use your imagination.

Supplies needed

Primer (I used Tamiya Buff and Medium Gray)

Flat White paint (I used Tamiya)

Dark Yellow, Dark Gray, Flat Earth, semigloss black paints (I used Tamiya)

Clear Gloss and thinner (Gunze Sangyo recommended)

LMG Pearl Powders (Yellow pearl and green-yellow pearl)

Burnt Umber and Black artist's oil paints

Mineral spirits paint thinner

Semigloss clear acrylic (AeroMaster recommended)

Distilled or filtered water

High-flow and fine airbrush nozzles

Fig. 2-1

One important note: for a vinyl figure, you must use mostly water-based acrylic paints. If you use enamels or lacquers on a vinyl kit, the paint will never dry, due to a chemical reaction between the vinyl and the paints. For this kit we will use acrylic paints exclusively, except for a little drybrush paint detailing.

Step 1: The primer coat

To get started, first assemble the model according to the kit instructions (see fig. 2-1). Note especially the putty on the seams and joints. Spend as much time as you need to make these look good. I used Squadron green putty to blend the seams and re-created the creature's scales, scars, and lines in the putty with curved circular and triangular-section riffler files, scribing tools, and sandpaper.

When the model is ready to paint, prepare your airbrush for the primer coat. Make sure the airbrush is clean; test it by running some clear thinner through it. Ideally, use a high-flow nozzle to apply the first primer coat. You can use a nozzle that is not high-flow, but it will take longer to build up the paint.

The primer I used here is a mixture of Tamiya Buff and Medium Gray. This gives the model a relatively neutral, medium tone to begin with. Mix your paint with enough thinner to give the consistency of milk, and test the spray pattern before spraying it on the model. Be sure to mix enough of this paint for this next step and also set some aside for later use.

Spray the model in several coats, being careful not to hold the airbrush in one place too long, which can cause the paint to "puddle" or run. Start with a few light coats over the entire model. As you add more paint, and the paint begins to dry, you can add successively heavier coats of paint to completely cover the model. This step takes only a short time—in just a few minutes, you should have the primer coat completed (see fig. 2-2).

Put the model in a warm, dry place to dry and clean the airbrush well. Drying time varies, but flat acrylic paints tend to dry rapidly.

Fig. 2-2. Prime the figure with a mixture of Tamiya acrylic Buff and Medium Gray as a basecolor for the entire model. Use only acrylic paints on vinyl models or parts, or the paint will never dry!

Step 2: The underside

Next, we'll add a lighter tone to the belly and underside of the creature. Mix some Tamiya Flat White into the earlier primer mixture (or mix it with Medium Gray if you've used up all the primer). You do not need to mix a tremendous amount of paint—roughly ¼ ounce or less should be enough.

If you have a fine needle and tip, install them at this point. You may want to decrease the pressure of your air source, to allow finer detailing and to avoid spraying too much paint onto the model. Either use a regulator to decrease the pressure or just loosen the connection of the air hose to the air source.

Spray the belly and underside of the model carefully, trying to keep the paint from covering areas where you don't want this lighter shade. You don't have to be overcautious, just observant. Hold the airbrush relatively close to the model; this allows finer detail without adding too much paint at once (see fig. 2-3).

When you are satisfied with the coverage of the lighter shade, put the model aside to dry for a while—and don't forget to clean the airbrush and run thinner through it to prepare for the next color. If possible, save some of your paint for future touchups.

Fig. 2-3. Paint the belly a lighter tone than the rest of the body.

Fig. 2-4. Using Dark Yellow to highlight certain areas gives the creature an added dimension of color.

Step 3: Adding a warm color

The next step adds a bit of warm color to the model. We will do that by using the fine tip installed on the airbrush to apply Tamiya Dark Yellow paint. As before, mix the paint to a milky consistency, then carefully spray the dark yellow mixture to the sides and darker areas of the model. Test the color on scrap paper or cardstock before adding it to the model.

Be careful to avoid covering the lighter shade on the underside you just finished. Work carefully, again decreasing the pressure to make the paint application smooth, light, and steady.

If you overdo the application of this color, you can go back to the earlier, lighter color and carefully "fog in" a touchup to the affected area, a relatively easy fix. Afterwards, clean the airbrush well and let the model dry. Figure 2-4 shows the model after this stage.

Step 4: Adding the dark color

The darkest colors on the creature are a mixture of Tamiya Semigloss Black, German Gray, and Flat Earth. Adjust the ratios of these colors as you see fit. The main idea is to have a dark color, but not as dark as black. The Flat Earth color gives the paint a warm earth tone that complements the other colors. This color and mixture do not have to be exact; use your own color sense and imagination to make it look right to you.

You will need to mix about ¼ to ½ oz. of paint for this step. Be sure to thin it to the right consistency. Test the spray pattern on cardstock. You will be painting relatively fine lines in this step; it is fairly easy with a little practice.

Hold the airbrush quite close to the model, and use as little air pressure as possible—just enough for the paint to smoothly exit onto the model in a very fine pattern (see fig. 2-5). Paint the top surfaces of the model, the spikes, and a number of narrow vertical stripes on the tail and over parts of the arms and legs.

Fig. 2-5. Apply a darker mixture with a fine nozzle for a striped effect, especially on the tail. It also adds depth and color to the spine and extremities without obliterating the layered colors underneath.

You may also want to add spots to the model. If your paint tip is fine enough and your hand is steady enough, you can spray the spots freehand. Try this technique on scrap material first. But if you want more control while painting spots, simply cut a mask: take a piece of card stock and punch a couple of different-sized holes into it (see fig. 2-7). Again, test this on scrap material first.

Hold the mask close to the model, but not touching it where the spot is to be located. Make sure there is roughly ¹⁄₁₆" clearance, as you do not want the spots too dark or hard-edged. It doesn't take a lot of paint to make the spots; just a few light passes over the hole will do the trick.

Figure 2-6 shows the model after you have finished these detailing steps. Applying the color for darker areas takes more time than earlier steps because the detail is finer, but the technique is loose (and fun!). Once you have finished, set the model aside to dry thoroughly, clean the airbrush, remove the fine tip, and install the high-flow tip for the next step.

Fig. 2-6. The creature looks very realistic after a few steps, when it has acquired a variety of colors and shades. Notice the effect of the airbrushed stripes and dots that mimic the skin colors and patterns on amphibians, reptiles, and dinosaurs.

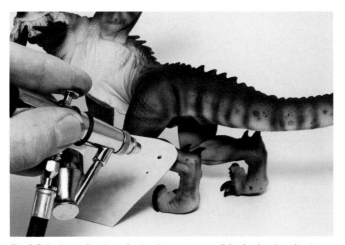

Fig. 2-7. Apply smaller dots of color that are too small for freehand application through a simple mask made from an index card.

Fig. 2-8. Once the airbrushed patterns are to your liking, seal the entire model with a clear coat. Sealing the underlying finish is necessary if you want to add color washes to the model for more realism.

Step 5: A protective coat

When your model has dried, it's time to apply a heavy clear-gloss acrylic coat. This will serve as a barrier coat to protect your completed airbrushing from the wash techniques we'll use after this to detail the model.

I've used Gunze Sangyo clear gloss, thinned with their house brand product, Mr. Thinner. It does not require a lot of thinner, just enough to help the paint flow well through your high-flow nozzle. Liberally apply the clear acrylic, being careful not to overdo it (filling in detail or making the paint run). But you can add a relatively wet coat quickly. Make sure you cover the entire model, holding the airbrush close to the model and applying quick strokes of your arm while applying the clear.

You may need to set the model aside to dry before painting all of the extremities, depending on how you hold the model while painting it. The clear gloss dries quickly. When finished, put any excess paint aside, saving it for a later coat. Clean the airbrush by running thinner through it. Figure 2-8 shows the clearcoated model.

Fig. 2-9. Simple paint washes, using oil-based artist's paints and thinners, add extra depth to your model after it's been airbrushed. This is an easy, fun step, contributing greatly to the dramatic feeling of the overall finish.

Fig. 2-10. Dry pearl powders are an excellent addition to your paint palette. You'll usually mix these pearls with clear to get a myriad of shimmering colors and effects when viewed under different lighting.

Step 6: Brush-painted details

When the clear coat is dry, you can add brush-painted details, such as a wash (see fig. 2-9). This wash is a mixture of artist's oil paints—a combination of black and burnt umber (dark brown with a hint of red)—and mineral spirits. It is applied liberally to the model with a wide brush. As it dries, use an old T-shirt to remove it from the high surfaces of the model, leaving most of the wash down in all the little crevices. You can do as many coats of wash as you wish.

You will notice that the wash changes the overall color of the model. This is an easy detail to add and gives the airbrushed work a new level of "life." Similar airbrush and wash techniques are commonly used by aircraft builders for both camouflage and panel line details, for example. At this point, you can also dry-brush highlights and paint teeth, eyes, and claws to your liking.

Step 7: A pearl effect

The technique I have used over the wash is well known to model car builders. I have added a slight, glimmering pearl effect to the scales, giving the model an extra level of realism. Figure 2-10 shows the materials used to mix the pearls. I used two shades of pearl: yellow, and a yellowish green. I started with the yellow, mixing a small amount into the previously mixed acrylic clear. I carefully misted the pearl onto the darkest parts of the model. Be careful not to add too much. Use the high-flow nozzle, and decrease your air pressure down if necessary. The pearl effect builds rapidly.

Once I had finished the pearl yellow coat, I then sprayed some of the pearl yellow-green mixture onto just the tops of the spikes and the scales closest to them. You can see the pearl effect in fig. 2-11. It really looks convincing. Clean the airbrush well, and let the model dry.

Fig. 2-11. The pearl added to the clear gives extra "life" and realism to the finish.

Step 7: Clear acrylic

After you have added the pearl coats and have finished any other brush-painting details, add another heavy coat of clear acrylic to the model and let it cure thoroughly. This seals all of the previous coats in place.

Fig. 2-12. The finished "Relic."

Step 8: Toning down the gloss

Finally, I wanted to bring down the level of gloss on the figure. In the movie, the creature was generally wet. However, for the model's most realistic appearance, I wanted a somewhat drier, less "wet" appearance—but not too flat, either. I chose to use a semigloss acrylic clear as my final coat.

I used AeroMaster Semigloss Clear to achieve this effect. Mix the paint with a few drops of distilled water. You can also add a couple drops of Windex to the mixture, or Polly-S thinner.

You will only need about ½ oz. or less of this mixture. Spray the semigloss paint over the model lightly, building it up slowly. You do not want this coat to have any tendency to crack as it dries over the gloss surface, so take your time building it up. You may want to hold your airbrush away from the model, spraying it with the nozzle fully open but from a distance of 6 to 10 inches away, so that the paint settles on the model very lightly.

As you spray the model, the glossiness will become less evident. If the model still seems too glossy, you could mix some AeroMaster flat clear into the mixture to tone down the gloss further. This paint dries rapidly. Once you are satisfied with the gloss level, set the model aside to dry. Clean the airbrush well.

You're done!

You are now finished with the model, unless you wish to add a few final small paint details.

This is a great way to learn how fun, easy, and loose a technique this is—and you have a model that looks quite realistic. I will give away a big secret. I was extremely pleased with the outcome of this model—and I had never practiced this particular series of techniques before.

If I could do this so easily the very first time, so can you. I hope you have as much fun building and painting your model as

I had. And you will enjoy showing the results of your airbrush experience to other modelers, just as I have.

Remember these techniques. They can just as easily be used on an armor model, on aircraft, on a dinosaur, or on a vehicle or creature with any kind of camouflage. The techniques used are basically the same. These great eye-catching results are easily achieved with great help from your airbrush—and your imagination.

This type of model does not require a huge commitment of time to achieve spectacular results. Your airbrush makes finishes like this fun to apply and easy to achieve.

3

The Hummer

Use Your Airbrush to Draw Camouflage Patterns on Your Model

Camouflage patterns are simple to paint with an airbrush. You can follow a pattern seen in a photograph, or you can be creative, selecting a scheme that suits your idea of the ideal pattern for your particular model.

This exercise will show how easy and fun it is to apply basic camouflage. The technique can be used to dress up any type of model you desire. I chose the Hummer because I wanted to make a replica of a civilian military-style vehicle with a desert-style camouflage pattern—a pattern that a "real" owner might want on his vehicle to make it stand out and be noticed.

You can use this technique to create patterns on any number of your aircraft or armor models.

Fig. 3-1. Here is the Humvee in a basic "raw canvas" state before camouflaging. The body and wheels are painted in Tamiya Desert Yellow acrylic.

Step 1: Base yellow

Start by painting the entire body with Tamiya Desert Yellow as the base color. This is the lightest color used in this camouflage pattern. Thin it appropriately for smooth flow, and apply it in uniform coats until the color is completely saturated. Clean the airbrush, and let the body dry.

Figure 3-1 shows the body and wheels painted in the Desert Yellow base color.

Step 2: Brown areas

Next, you'll paint the brown areas. First, mask off the roof and deck panels, which will be simulated vinyl without a camouflage pattern. Mix roughly equal parts of Flat Earth and Red Brown until you are satisfied with the color. Thin the mixture appropriately and apply it with a fine-tip nozzle.

Figure 3-2 shows the application of the color panels. I started by outlining the colored areas and then filled them in slowly and carefully. You can do this completely freehand without masking. I used a magazine photo for rough reference.

Apply the paint with the airbrush held very close to the surface of the model, as you are using the airbrush to draw the paint pattern directly on the model. You can be as exacting as you want—or as loose as you want. Clean the airbrush, and you are ready for the next step.

Figure 3-3 shows the model with the completed brown camouflage panels.

Step 3: Olivegrün

The Olivegrün color is next. Thin it and apply it in the same way as the previous brown color. Add these color sections carefully and slowly. As with the previous steps in painting camouflage, hold the airbrush close to the surface and use it like an air-powered drawing instrument. Once you are satisfied with the green pattern, remove the roof and deck masking, clean the airbrush, and let the body dry.

Figure 3-4 shows the basic model with the completed camouflage panels, along with the paints used to achieve the colors.

Fig. 3-2. You can add the camouflage pattern freehand with a fine-detail airbrush. Notice how close you can get to precisely "draw" the camouflage outline directly onto the model.

Step 4: Last details

I wanted the vinyl top and deck covering to be a slightly lighter shade than the previous Desert Tan. So I mixed together equal parts of Desert Tan and Buff for the desired color. Then, I mixed the paint with rubbing alcohol as the thinner; this creates a flatter sheen than Tamiya's thinner.

After carefully masking the body (see fig. 3-5), I applied the mixture to the top.

Figure 3-6 shows the completed paint job, including a few other elements, such as the black trim panels, that I brush-painted as well.

At this point, you may want to apply a coat of flat clear to protect the previous colors. This coat will also give a uniform, dull appearance to the entire model.

Fig. 3-3. With the addition of sections painted with a mixture of Tamiya Flat Earth and Red Brown, the camouflage pattern is halfway complete.

Fig. 3-4. Add AeroMaster Olivegrün as the next camouflage color. Here, the model shows off its finished camouflage pattern, with the colors used to achieve the effect.

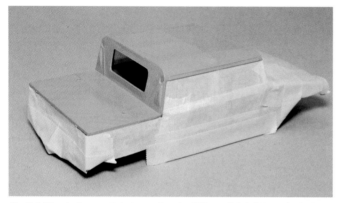

Fig. 3-5. The vinyl top and deck covering should be a slightly lighter shade than the previous Desert Yellow. Mask off the camouflaged areas, and spray a mixture of Desert Yellow and Buff to achieve the correct shade.

Fig. 3-6. The finished paint job was very easy to apply and was quick to dry. A simple model like this is an easy way to familiarize yourself with camouflage techniques. Once you've tried it, you can quickly move on toward more intricate camouflage patterns on any subject.

That's it!

That's all it takes for a great camouflage finish! The camouflage paint, with other details and assembly, took only a few short hours to accomplish, and I was quite satisfied with the results. The flat acrylics dry very quickly; this lets you accomplish a lot of paint details in a short amount of time.

Trying these techniques on a simple snap-kit is a fun way to learn how to paint a camouflage pattern. After this, you'll want to tackle more challenging paint schemes on aircraft and armor models with your airbrush.

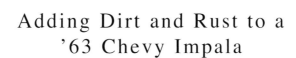

Adding Dirt and Rust to a
'63 Chevy Impala

The following exercise will show you how easy it is to add realistic weathering to models with your airbrush. There are a number of techniques you can use to achieve weathered finishes; some of those are well-documented in Pat Covert's book, *The Modeler's Guide to Scale Automotive Finishes* (Kalmbach Publishing Co.).

While pastels and real dirt are common weathering materials, you can apply a more permanent dirty, weathered finish with your airbrush. You control the amount of "dirt" by controlling the paint colors, mixtures, and amounts applied to the surfaces. It is relatively easy and a lot of fun to do.

Don't worry about precise application or color match. Just get close, stay "loose," and have fun.

Fig. 4-1. Here's the basic chassis detail, painted before adding weathering. The weathering will cover up a lot of fine paint details, so your colors and finishes need not be exact or precise.

Step 1: Painting the model

Paint the body on this '63 Impala using a combination of flat acrylics: a rust-colored primer overall, highlighted with a few areas of light gray primer for touchups. First paint the chassis with flat black, and then detail it with brush-painted engine, transmission, and exhaust details (see fig. 4-1).

You can be as exacting as you want with the colors. But realistically, once the model has been "dirtied," all the colors blend together, so your chassis detail colors don't need to be especially precise before you apply the weathering.

Step 2: Add the rust

The first step in weathering the chassis is to add a fine mist of Model Master Rust acrylic paint to the chassis. Figure 4-2 shows a light, general application of the paint. You can use a medium or heavy tip.

You want to mist the paint on rather "dry," so don't hold the airbrush too close. Start at about a foot away, and adjust the distance until you are happy with the results. This step will go quickly, and the rust color dries rapidly as well.

You may not need to thin the paint for this detail. But if the unthinned paint does not flow from your airbrush, thin it just enough for it to flow out in a grainy pattern.

Step 3: Add the "dirt"

The next step is to add the "dirt" color to the chassis. Use any acrylic flat color in the tan range. Some colors are actually made to resemble earth; just choose your favorite. The color shown in fig. 4-3 is Polly S Rust, which is actually a good earth tone.

Apply this color using the same method as the rust. You may want to direct the dirt rearward, however, giving more of the paint buildup to the front-facing surfaces of chassis and wheel wells, to simulate the motion and direction of dirt being sprayed onto the chassis. Just focus on aiming your airbrush as you apply paint toward the rear of the car in general.

This coat covers quickly. You can apply a light coat to simulate a newer car, or a heavier coat as shown here to create an older car or truck. It's easy to overdo this weathering on a "newer" vehicle. To keep the dirty color from building up too rapidly, you can mix up to half of the color with acrylic flat clear. This will reduce the overall dirt-color saturation. With very little practice, you will easily master this effect with your airbrush.

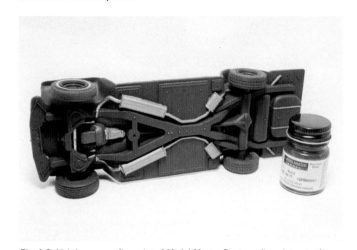

Fig. 4-2. Lightly spray a fine mist of Model Master Rust acrylic paint onto the chassis as the first step toward a weathered airbrush finish.

Step 4: Spraying the body

Save the remaining "dirt" mix to apply to the body—or mix your favorite acrylic dirt color for the body. If you haven't already, you'll want to thin the paint a bit with some flat clear acrylic paint and test the pattern first. Generally, spray more heavily on the lower side panels, more lightly as you go over the top of the model.

I masked the windshield wiper paths (see fig. 4-5). After applying the "dirt," I removed the mask, resulting in a very accurate-looking dirty windshield with wiper marks in place.

Notice the windshield tint strip (see fig. 4-4), added with a fine-line detail airbrush. This little detail really sets a model apart, and is best replicated with an airbrush rather than decals or any other means. I like to use transparent blue and green enamel colors from spray cans for this, spraying the paint from the cans carefully into my airbrush jar. Then I apply this paint directly with the fine tip airbrush to the windshield. No thinning of the paint should be necessary, and the enamel "bites" into the clear plastic with ease. Hold the nozzle quite close to the surface, and gently apply the paint in a side-to-side motion as if you are drawing the pattern onto the top of the windshield.

Fig. 4-3. Follow up the first layer of rust by spraying a light coat of an earth-tone "dirt" color. Any earth-tone color that simulates dirt will work.

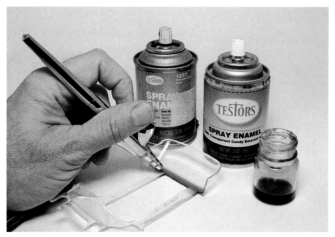

Fig. 4-4. Painting the dark tint strip across the top of a windshield adds realism to any car model. It is easy to apply using an airbrush with a fine nozzle.

Fig. 4-5. Add an overall dirty appearance by lightly spraying the entire model with some of the "dirt" mixture used previously on the chassis. Mask the windshield first to simulate accurate "wiper paths."

The effect is very realistic. To finish the tint strip, let the windshield dry thoroughly, and then remove any overspray with a soft cloth and plastic polish by buffing the surface.

I prefer to use Novus no. 2 to polish the windshield. This completely cleans and shines the windshield, leaving a perfect in-scale faded tint strip.

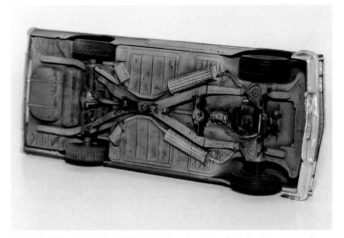

Fig. 4-6. Add a drybrushed "oil" stain after the airbrushed dirt for extra realism. Even though this is only paint on plastic, it sure has the "feel" of grimy, greasy dirt, typical of almost every old car.

Fig. 4-7. The finished model shows a lot of realism achieved with little effort, using an airbrush and flat-finish acrylic paints.

That's it!

The photos above show the body and chassis after the air-brushed weathering has been applied to both. The appearance is quite realistic. You can stop at this point, or further detail your model with washes, pastels, or other finishes added on top of the paint (see figs. 4-6 and 4-7).

Use your imagination. Remember, you can use the chassis weathering shown here for all car models. Once a car has been driven a few months, the chassis is covered in a uniform film of dirt and road grime.

Easily added to your models with an airbrush, this touch will make your models far more realistic.

5

Star Wars® X-Wing

Use Your Airbrush to Add Great Details to a Simple Snap-Together Kit

An airbrush allows you to add details to science-fiction models that are difficult to achieve with other methods, such as weathering effects and portraying a history of "hits." A myriad of panels with slightly different colors is also easy to create.

These airbrushed details will help to make your science-fiction model look much more realistic.

This project is a simple Star Wars X-Wing Fighter. The model is a basic snap-kit with average detail. Even a model as simple as this really benefits from some airbrush weathering.

And it's a good way to learn some basic techniques before you move on to building and painting kits with higher levels of detailing.

Supplies needed

Tamiya Neutral Gray

Tamiya Dark Gray

Testors Gunmetal Buffing Metalizer

Tamiya Flat Yellow

Tamiya Buff

Gunze Clear Gloss

AeroMaster Flat Clear

Step 1: Getting started

Begin building the model by putting together the basic sub-assemblies as outlined in the directions. Then cover them with a coat of flat white paint or white primer. Flat white is fine, but primer will cover the plastic faster and easier. Next, add an acrylic clear coat over the white primer. When it has dried, apply the decals. Decals can be weathered by scratching bits of damage with a fingernail (see fig. 5-1).

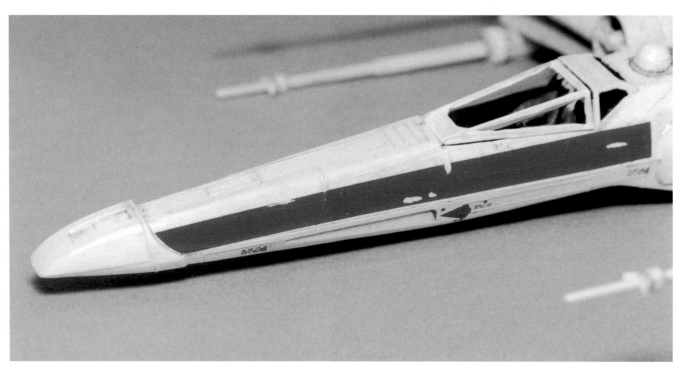

Fig. 5-1. Here is the model—assembled, primed, sealed with clear, with color decals added. Notice the battle damage added for effect.

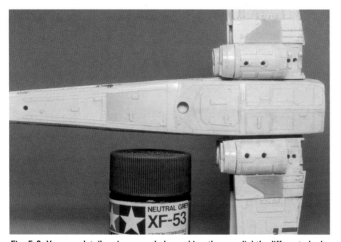

Fig. 5-2. You can detail various panels by making them a slightly different shade than their surroundings. Create this panel effect by masking the panels and spraying a very light application of Tamiya Neutral Gray.

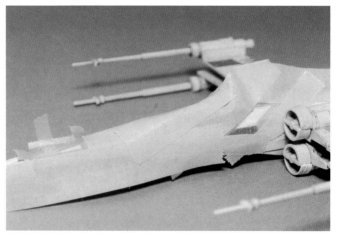

Fig. 5-3. Here are some of the panels, masked and ready to be sprayed with a color that contrasts with the surrounding area.

Step 2: Enhance the look

Your airbrush is a great tool to enhance the overall look of the model. In fig. 5-2, several panels underneath (and on top as well) have been detailed with a few light coats of Tamiya Neutral Gray.

Notice the fogged panel towards the left, just above the bottle. Little details like this are quick and easy to do with an airbrush, and the reward is a very realistic finish. Use a fine nozzle if possible.

Figure 5-3 shows some other panels masked off. Paint these panels with a light coat of Buff mixed with Flat Yellow (see fig. 5-4). Add only a faint layer of this color over the white base.

Next, mask a series of top panels (fig. 5-5) and shoot them with a light mist of Neutral Gray. Figure 5-6 shows the results.

Step 3: Add a wash

After applying all the airbrush panels, you can add your favorite oil or enamel-based wash with a brush (see fig. 5-7). This brings out highlights and is easily cleaned up and smeared around with a rag. Keep it loose and have fun. Notice how the wash settles into the small details on the top and adds a distinctly grimy appearance to the model in general.

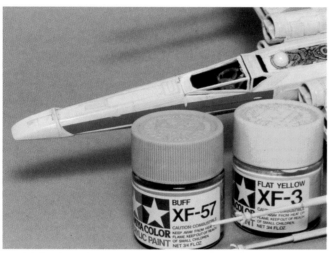

Fig. 5-4. Use Tamiya Buff and Flat Yellow sparingly to add a little color to various panels for extra detail.

Fig. 5-5. Here are additional areas, masked and ready for panels to be colored.

Fig. 5-6. Here are the results—a nice effect, don't you think, with the variety of contrasting panel colors?

Fig. 5-7. Before building and detailing, seal your model in clear acrylic paint. This allows you to apply oil-based washes to the surfaces without damaging the paint and decals underneath.

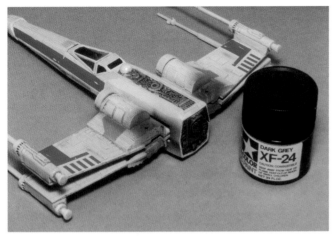

Fig. 5-8. Exhaust burns and "hits" are easy to create by carefully spraying Tamiya Dark Gray to the appropriate areas. This adds a lot of realism and life to an otherwise simple model kit.

Fig. 5-9. Airbrush the engines with a combination of Testors Gunmetal Metalizer toward the rear, fading from Tamiya Dark Gray at the front inlet area.

Step 4: Engine exhaust burns and "hits"

Now you can tackle the engine exhaust burns and "hits" caused by flying, burning debris (see fig. 5-8). You don't need to mask the parts. Just apply the Dark Gray color around where the engines mount. Hold the airbrush close to the model, at about a 45-degree angle, and gently spray small "hits" to the surface with a momentary push of the airbrush trigger. You can also use flat black paint acrylic paint for this step if you want the burn marks to look even darker.

Assemble the engines, and paint them in Dark Gray towards the inlet side, gradually fading to a metalizer gunmetal shade towards the exhaust end (see fig. 5-9). You can install the engines once they're dry.

Step 5: Add a protective coat

When you are happy with the painted weathering, overcoat the entire model with flat clear acrylic. Be sure to mask the canopy (see fig. 5-10). After applying the flat clear, you can add further brush-painted details. I brought out the finish of the airbrushed engine and other raised mechanical areas by using a drybrushed mixture of white and silver enamel paints.

It's amazing how easy it is!

Figures 5-11 through 5-13 show the finished model. It is amazing how quickly you can do realistic weathering using your airbrush. Start with simple models. Once you have learned the techniques, you will soon tackle complex weathering and detailing with ease, applying them with expert results.

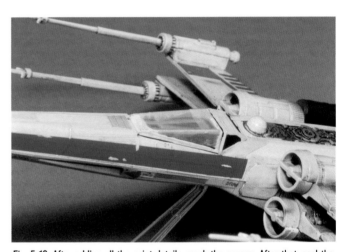

Fig. 5-10. After adding all the paint details, mask the canopy. After that, seal the entire model with a flat clear mixture (to dull down and smooth out the previously applied paint).

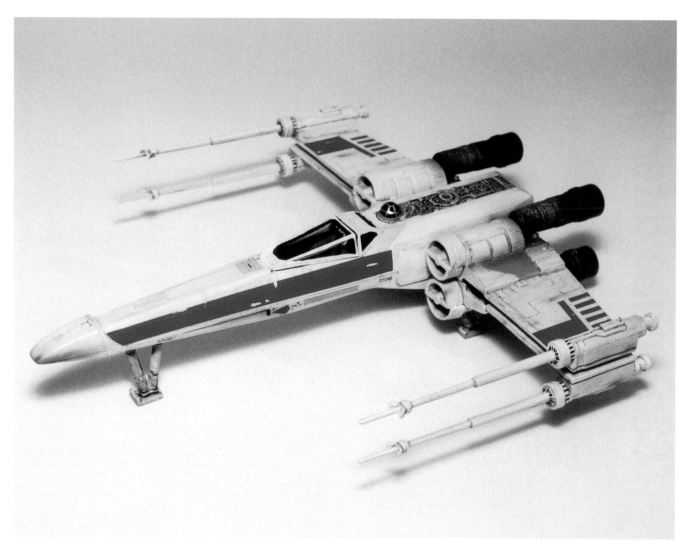

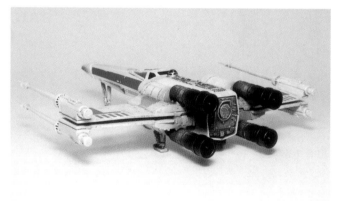

Figs. 5-11 to 5-13. For such a simple kit, the paint details really make it stand out from the crowd. Now, it looks far more interesting than just the sum of its parts. And best of all—it was fun and easy to do!

6

'62 Pontiac Interior

Airbrushing a Flamboyant Interior for a '62 Pontiac Catalina

Many cars from the '50s and '60s had striking, colorful interiors. With an airbrush, you can paint one of these eye-catching, show-stopping interiors on a model and realistically match the actual colors used.

Or you can creatively alter the colors as you see fit.

For this project, we will create a tri-tone interior on AMT's 1962 Pontiac Catalina that closely matches that of the real car. The tri-tone interior was part of the Ventura trim option; the interior we'll replicate is primarily red. You can use the same approach to create an interior in blue or any other range of colors.

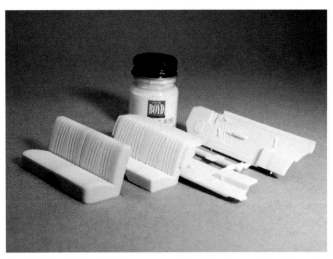

Fig. 6-1. Prime the basic interior components in white. Some of the white parts will be visible on the finished car.

This project uses a combination of enamels and acrylics; however, you can use only enamels or acrylics, if you wish.

Step 1: Prep work

Begin by separating the model's parts from the trees. Clean up mold lines and trim points. You may wish to paint the parts in subassemblies for easier handling.

Glue the seatbacks to the front seat, fill the seam with gap-filling super glue, and sand the seam smooth once it's dry. Next, clean the parts with warm, soapy water and let them dry thoroughly.

Step 2: A white primer coat

The first step in painting is to prime the interior parts (see fig. 6-1). I painted the seats and door panels with Testors Colors by Boyd White Primer, thinned to a milky consistency.

This primer is used as the base coat for all subsequent colors. It is also the actual color for several sections of the interior: on the door panels (the small diagonal stripe) and the center portion of the seats.

Apply the primer with your airbrush, using either a high- or a medium-flow tip. Clean the airbrush thoroughly afterwards.

Mask the primed seats and door panels (fig. 6-2). Cover the areas that are to stay white with masking tape. Burnish the tape in place and trim it with a hobby knife. Figure 6-2 also shows Testors Dullcote lacquer.

Step 3: A protective coat

After masking the seats, mix the Dullcote with the appropriate thinner and spray the masked areas. Do not spray this mixture too lightly—but also try to avoid applying so much that it obliterates

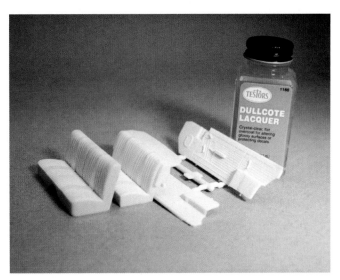

Fig. 6-2. Use Dullcote Lacquer to give a satin sheen to either gloss or flat interior colors. It is also good at sealing the edges of masking tape, so colored paint applied over it will not bleed through.

detail. A high-flow tip will work; just be careful to keep the paint from flowing too heavily. Adjust the pressure accordingly, or if you are using a single-action brush, practice first and figure out the correct distance at which to spray to get the right application.

This step will keep the red paint that you will apply in the next step from bleeding through the masking. Again, clean the airbrush thoroughly with thinner.

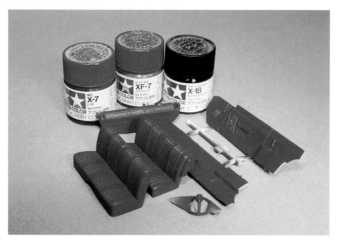

Fig. 6-3. The interior color is a bit darker than plain red. To match the color, carefully add a few drops of black to the mixture. Mixing flat and gloss paints can help achieve a satin finish that looks like vinyl.

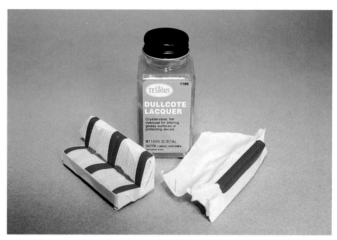

Fig. 6-4. You will paint several areas a dark shade of maroon. Carefully mask the previously painted areas and as before, seal the edges with clear to avoid bleed-through of the colored paint.

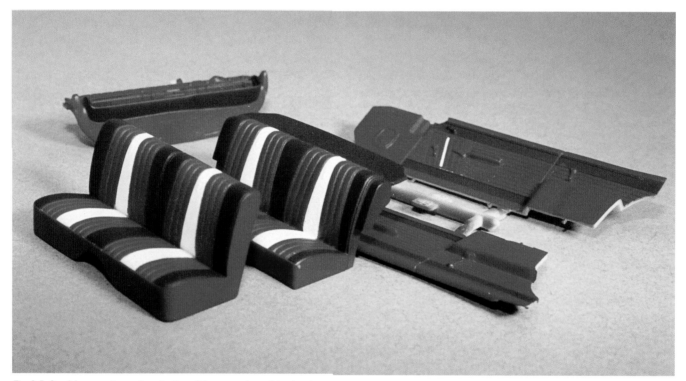

Fig. 6-5. Careful preparation and application of the successive paint colors is evident on these finished parts, ready for final assembly.

Step 4: Adding the red color

The next step is to paint the second color, in this case a medium-to-dark red. This color is mixed using equal parts of Tamiya Gloss and Flat Red, plus a few drops of Semigloss Black to darken. Be careful adding the black; it is easy to overdo it. Add the appropriate amount of thinner. I used this mix of flat, gloss, and semigloss paints to achieve a vinyl-like finish. Automotive vinyl has a semigloss sheen, so mixing flat and gloss paints gives the right balance.

Instead, you could use a gloss color, then overcoat it with Dullcote (or a mixture of clear gloss and Dullcote to achieve a semigloss sheen). Or, if you started with a flat color, you could overcoat it with a semigloss mixture of Dullcote and clear gloss.

Figure 6-3 shows the seats, door panels, dash, and steering wheel painted in the red mixture. Notice the masking on the steering wheel; this particular wheel is molded in clear, with the spokes and hand locations painted in red.

After painting the parts, set them aside to dry thoroughly before you begin the final step in the painting process. Remember to clean the airbrush again.

Step 5: The last color

The final step to the Catalina's tri-tone color theme is to paint appropriate areas in dark maroon. This includes the dashboard, a horizontal stripe on the door panels, and the outboard panels on the front and rear seats.

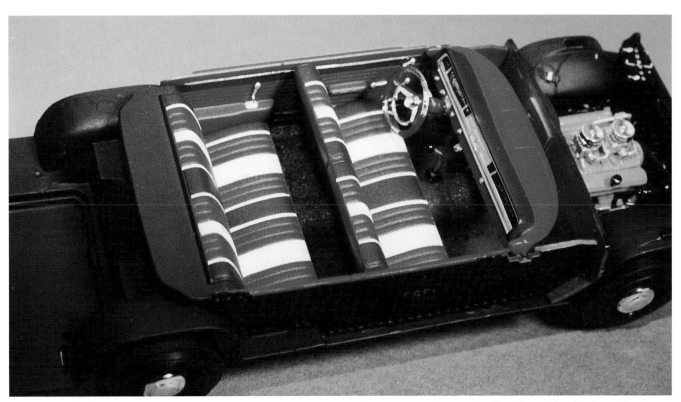

Fig. 6-6. The finished interior, before final assembly of the entire model. A few paint details using authentic colors–and application of decals, foil, and flocking– add up to a very realistic interior without the need for a lot of expensive after-market parts.

Begin by masking the seats, dash, and door panels. Trim the excess tape with a hobby knife. Again use the Dullcote mixture to prevent color bleed (see fig. 6-4).

After applying the Dullcote, spray the dark maroon. To mix this color, start with the red previously used on the interior, and slowly add drops of semigloss black until you reach the desired shade of maroon. Then thin appropriately. Spray this on the parts carefully, let dry, and remove the masking (see fig. 6-5).

If at this point the finish is either too glossy or too dull, you can overcoat it with gloss clear, Dullcote, or a mixture of the two for the proper sheen. I have seen many model car interiors that were well painted and detailed, but the seats were either too shiny or too dull. This is so easy to fix. And the level of realism that you get with the correct sheen will set your models apart from the rest.

With an airbrush, you have the control needed to build up the proper sheen in the paint finish—something difficult if not impossible to do with spray cans or paint brushes.

Step 6: Add any last details

After painting the interior, you can detail it to your liking (see fig. 6-6). I've added Bare Metal Foil and various brush-painted details to the dash and the door panels. I also used thin white decals to mimic the white piping on the seats where the red and maroon panels meet. It was easier to apply these decals than to mask and paint the piping. But if you have no decal material, you can mask the piping too.

Notice the clear steering wheel. I added extra detail by lightly tinting it with a light coat of clear yellow gloss acrylic applied with a paintbrush. It's faster and easier to do this detail with a brush, since the acrylic smooths out and does not show brushmarks.

The final touch before assembly was to flock the carpeting a matching shade of red. Looks pretty convincing, doesn't it?

The multicolored interior gives nice contrast and an authentic look to the finished jet-black model.

Bringing a model to life

While the masking and painting is time-consuming, the multi-color effect really brings the interior alive. This is relatively easy to achieve with patience and determination. Using your airbrush allows you to exactly match colors—and apply them in a far more controlled fashion than from spray cans. And you will have used so little paint that you haven't obliterated any detail, allowing the finely engraved seat patterns to show through.

Other than the use of flocking, this interior is completely paint-detailed from the box and could hold its own against interiors using more detail parts. Imagine how realistic it could look by adding more details: photoetched keys, seatbelts, aftermarket decals, and other small parts. The colorful treatment really adds to the overall appearance of the basic "Tuxedo Black" model.

Following proper notes makes a difference. For this project, I took copious notes when visiting a museum that had one of these Catalinas on display. Even with detailed notes, however, it is possible to make mistakes. If you are a Pontiac enthusiast who knows this car well, you will notice that I've painted the dashboard incorrectly. I painted the dash pad (upper portion) maroon, and the rest of the dash red. Unfortunately, I transposed the colors on the dashboard, and didn't notice this until I rechecked my notes—after the model was finished and glued together permanently.

Learn from my mistake: paint the upper portion, or pad, of the dash red, mask it off, and then paint the rest maroon. I know some of you will notice this small detail, and I want you to be able to recreate this model as accurately as possible. Take careful notes, and check them often!

7

Trans Am Camaro

Use Your Airbrush to Create a Wild-Colored Camaro

uilding an authentic replica of a wild-colored racing car may seem a daunting challenge, but it's easy when painted with an airbrush. Our subject for this project is Revell's Trans Am Camaro kit, which has been issued in several different color and team variations.

After seeing the vivid, multicolored paint scheme used on the Trans Am Camaro by Jamie Galles's team, and then discovering the availability of Slixx aftermarket decals for this particular variation, I was hooked.

Even better, MCW Automotive Finishes offers all the colors used on this car for the model hobbyist. MCW's

paints are automotive lacquers, mixed and thinned for use by modelmakers. They require special preparation, but are a pleasure to work with. Unlike enamels, lacquers etch into themselves after each coat. The top coat actually becomes part of the bottom coat through a chemical reaction.

These types of paints are very durable, but you must wear protective breathing apparatus while working with them—they emit strong, hazardous fumes during painting and while they're drying. Make sure you paint in a well-ventilated area. A spray booth where the paint fumes are filtered and exhausted outdoors is ideal.

Supplies needed

Camaro Trans Am racer kit by Revell
MCW 1016 Gray Acrylic Sealer
MCW 1004 Light Gray Primer
MCW 2001 White
MCW 2083 Blue
MCW 2082 Yellow
MCW 2067 Red
MCW 2160 Burple
MCW 1017 Clear
MCW 1003 Thinner
Slixx 1130 decal sheet

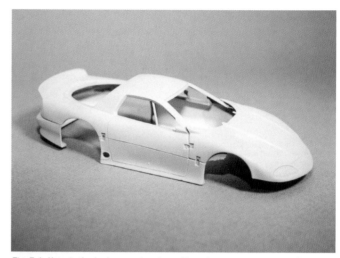

Fig. 7-1. Here is the body, seen in primer. The primer coat covers a sealer coat, which is necessary to prevent color bleed-through from the molded plastic color.

Fig. 7-2. The Trans Am Camaro body with its coat of gloss white lacquer.

Once you have dealt safely with that hazard, you are ready to complete a fine paint job with your airbrush. The results you'll get with this tool are fantastic. The fogged edges between the colors will be completely smooth, and there will be absolutely no line between colors or any grain to the paint where it is fogged.

Step 1: Seal and prime the plastic

Begin by prepping the body. Make sure to remove mold lines and clean the body of all fingerprints and mold-release agents or other residue.

First, you must apply a sealer coat to the plastic body. This shields the body from the strong lacquer paint and prevents the color of the plastic from bleeding through. I used a blue Camaro model; the same basic kit is also molded in yellow in other variations. Both of these colors will bleed profusely through all layers of your lacquer paint if you don't use the sealer.

After applying the sealer, you must wait at least one hour—and no longer than four hours—before applying the primer coat. If the sealer sits longer than four hours, you must reapply it before priming, so be ready to continue within the four-hour time span if possible.

MCW paints are prethinned and normally do not require additional thinning. Use a high-flow nozzle if possible to apply the lacquer. The lacquer can appear quite dull when applied (not a major problem at this point, though); a high-flow nozzle makes the paint go on a bit shinier. It is a good idea to have MCW thinner on hand, in case you need to add a few drops to the mixture to make the paint flow more easily. Remember, practice spraying the paint before painting the model! Figure 7-1 shows the body after it has been sealed and primed.

After priming the model, let it dry awhile—at least overnight, unless you speed up the drying with a dehydrator. Spray some thinner through the airbrush to clean it thoroughly.

Step 2: Gloss white basecoat

The next step is to paint the entire body in MCW Gloss White (fig. 7-2). This color will show on the nose and the bottom surfaces of the car. It is also a basecoat for the fogged colors. Apply it with smooth strokes of your arm, in a fluid back-and-forth motion, holding the tip of the airbrush perpendicular to the surface you are painting. Clean the airbrush. Let this coat dry overnight, and you're ready to proceed with the other colors.

Step 3: The first color: blue

The first color to spray is blue (see fig. 7-3). This color is located on the hood and part of the front bumper sides. You do not need to mask the white basecoat; just be careful to avoid painting heavily over the white as you get nearer to the nose, until you have a smooth blended area between the colors. Spray from the back of the hood forward.

Don't worry if you go overboard with the blue—you can always blend a bit of white back to the nose, being careful not to overdo it. (I had to do this, and you couldn't see where I did, as the paint blends into itself so nicely.) Clean the airbrush again.

Step 4: Next: yellow

Now you're ready to add the other colors to the body. First, mask the lower portions of the body sides that will remain white. Also mask the rear cowl area between the taillights (see fig. 7-4).

You can now apply the MCW Yellow, using the same technique as you did with the white (see fig. 7-4).

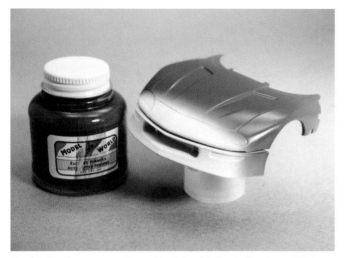

Fig. 7-3. The first step to achieve a blended multicolored effect is to add blue to the nose of the model, carefully fogging the paint toward the front and leaving the nose white.

Fig. 7-4. Next, add the yellow area at the back of the model, making sure you cover the areas to be blended into red.

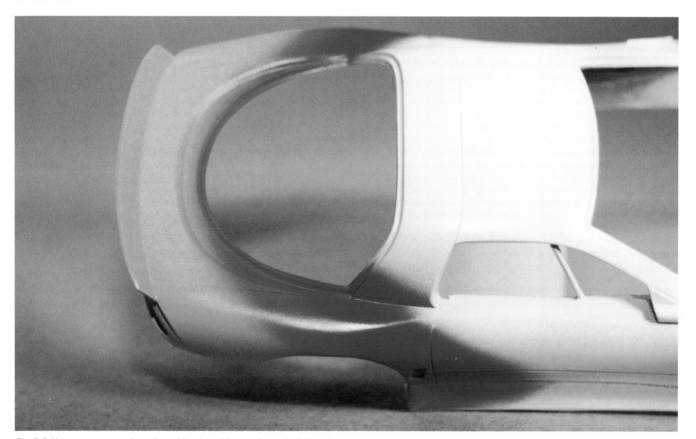

Fig. 7-5. Here you can see where the red has been blended, forward of the yellow section. The blended area looks orange. You can enhance this effect by mixing a bit of red with the yellow and carefully blending it into the area between the two colors.

Step 5: Add the red

After the yellow is on and you've cleaned the airbrush with thinner, go directly to the red. In fig. 7-5, I've sprayed the red carefully over the edge of the yellow, and forward onto the body. Again, if any red splatters too far onto the yellow, you can reshoot that area of yellow, blending it in until you are satisfied.

Try to be relatively loose while painting, moving the airbrush in a fluid motion, back and forth with your whole arm, with the tip always perpendicular (at a 90-degree angle) to the model surface.

If you want the transition from red to yellow to really stand out, you can mix the two colors and lightly fog this in between the two colors, giving a nice orange transition shade. It's really quite simple.

Fig. 7-6. The final color to add is Burple, which fills the entire area between the blue and red painted sections. Afterward, you can add a final clearcoat to the model (after it has dried overnight).

Step 6: Burple

After spraying the red and cleaning the airbrush yet again, proceed directly to the last color: Burple. Spray this over the entire roof, down the pillars, and over most of the door. It even covers the rear portion of the front fenders, from the front axle center line back.

Once you have finished with the Burple paint, clean the airbrush and let the model dry overnight. Then, remove all the masking and add a couple coats of MCW Clear to help blend the colors together and give the model some gloss.

Do make sure you spend time cleaning your airbrush between every coat, and after your final clear coat as well. You may be tired after a painting session and be tempted to clean it at a later date, but you must do it immediately, or you run the risk that paint will dry within the components. This would make it difficult if not impossible to clean the airbrush correctly and would affect its future performance, interfering with the flow of paint and air and causing premature wear on the components.

Step 7: A little polishing

If the paint appears a bit dull at this point, don't worry. Lacquers routinely dry dull after being sprayed through an airbrush, but they come alive to a high gloss when polished. After the clear has dried, polish it with your favorite polishing kit or automotive polish/wax. The final color and finish on this model turned out glass-smooth—amazing, considering this fogged/blended effect can turn other types of paint grainy, making a smooth final finish impossible.

Figure 7-6 shows the final color as applied, set upon the assembled chassis. In fig. 7-7, see how the colors match the photos of the real car. Now you can finish the model: applying the decals and completing the chassis and other details.

Lots of fun to finish

Normally, I do not build racing cars, yet this one turned out pretty well in my eyes. It has become one of my favorite models, receiving a lot of attention wherever it is shown. Figure 7-8

Fig. 7-7. I used magazine photos as color and decal reference guides for the painting and building process. The model matches the photos nicely.

Fig. 7-8. Voilà! The finished model, next to the Slixx decals I used.

Fig. 7-9. The finished model is quite striking. And the paint job was not difficult at all–with the proper tools and materials!

shows the car displayed with the Slixx decals. Without an airbrush, this project would have been much harder to paint. The fogged transitions would never have been as fine in this scale.

Once you try a project like this, beware! You may forever alter your building style, plunging gleefully into new, uncharted territory. For something more unusual, you could easily apply this paint scheme and graphics onto a model of a street-driven Camaro.

Now, that would really turn some heads.

8

Toyota Celica

Create an Award-winning
Finish on a Custom Car

A custom car model is a great place to show your talent at airbrushing. Cool graphic treatments are relatively easy, using your airbrush each step of the way. To some extent, techniques like these can be achieved in other ways, but you will get best results with your airbrush, employing the techniques I'll explain in this chapter.

My choice for a car on which to do some easy, eyecatching graphics is a Toyota Celica kit by Tamiya, which features modern, new-edge styling. To me, the car looks very Ford-like (basically a Toyota pony car, if you will). So in the spirit of customization, I'll unashamedly "borrow" a basic paint scheme (with minor variations) and wheels from a Revell model: the Mustang Super Stallion concept car.

I have added a few custom details to the body for a more balanced look, namely air intakes below the headlights and some lower-body cladding, fashioned from half-round sections of styrene strips.

I also have added a parts-box rear spoiler, featuring carbon-fiber constructions and scratchbuilt end plates.

White primer (Testors Colors by Boyd White Primer)

Gloss White paint (Testors enamel)

Gloss Yellow paint

Clear Gloss paint

True Blue pearl paint

Copenhagen blue

Masking tape (Tamiya fine-line tape and commercial masking tape)

Newspaper

LMG pearl white powder

LMG pearl yellow powder

High-flow airbrush nozzle

Fig. 8-1. The basic body with finished custom body treatments, primed in white.

Step 1: A primer coat

First, prepare the body for primer. Clean it and remove any mold lines, add custom details, and so on. Mix the white primer with Testors airbrush thinner (roughly a 50:50 mixture), until it is the consistency of milk. Next, spray the entire model with a few light coats of primer.

Start with a fairly light coat. Build the beginning coats of primer slowly at first. Hold the airbrush about 6 inches from the model, perpendicular to the surface you are painting. Use fluid strokes of your arm, back and forth in a smooth, even manner, over each surface of the model as the paint builds up. Start the flow of paint before one end of the model, and continue the flow beyond the other end.

You want the paint to flow smoothly. If it appears to be at all grainy, add a small amount of thinner to the paint mixture to get it to flow properly. As always, it is good to test this on another surface, such as a scrap body, before beginning on your model. The primer should cover relatively quickly. Once it has completely covered the surface and is smooth, put the body aside to dry (see fig. 8-1).

Next, apply primer to the chassis. Most unit-bodied chassis on cars are not completely painted. Usually, they are primed, and the body color is fogged onto the chassis' side surfaces from the outside inward. The center of the chassis often remains mostly just primer.

The kit chassis is molded in gray and looks enough like actual gray primer, so the white primer we are adding from the sides is for the effect of fogged-on body color.

Spray the chassis with white primer, holding the airbrush at

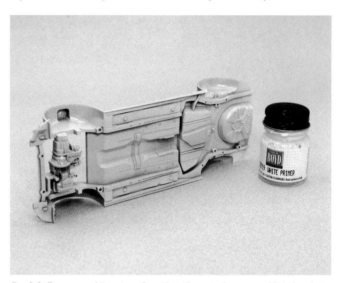

Fig. 8-2. Fog some white primer from the sides onto the gray-molded chassis to get an authentic "factory" oversprayed appearance.

about a 45-degree angle to the bottom surface. Cover the outside edges thoroughly, leaving the inner surfaces with a much thinner coat (see fig. 8-2 for the fogging effect).

Each successive coat of white paint added to the body during subsequent steps will be fogged onto the chassis. You don't have to be very careful or precise with this part of the paint application, unless you are going for a full-custom effect on a car not intended for driving on the street.

Fig. 8-3. Gloss white is the base color for this model. It will allow subsequent colors to appear as bright and vivid as possible.

Fig. 8-4. Use Tamiya masking tape for clean color separation lines and overall ease of use.

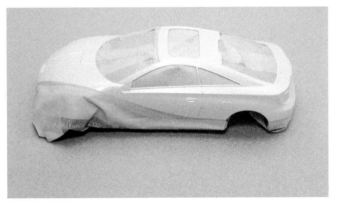

Fig. 8-5. Thoroughly mask off all areas that you won't cover in yellow.

Fig. 8-6. Airbrush clear enamel onto the tape edges to prevent color bleed-through.

Step 2: A white base coat

Now paint the base coat of the car white. Mix gloss white enamel with thinner to a milky consistency, and test the pattern to make sure it flows well. Using the same technique as for the primer coat, spray the body holding the airbrush perpendicular to the surface. Start with an overall light coat and slowly build up successive coats until they are smooth and you have achieved complete coverage and color saturation (see fig. 8-3).Once this is accomplished, set the model aside to dry.

Make sure all of the separate parts—such as mirrors and spoilers—are covered with the same number of coats as the body! And don't forget to clean the airbrush well with thinner once you've finished.

Step 3: A yellow coat

Your next step is to add the yellow paint. First, thoroughly mask all parts of the body to remain white (see fig. 8-4). I used Tamiya masking tape for the first layer of masking. It works well for masking custom paint schemes; it settles into the body panel lines nicely, conforms well to curves, and is easily removed when you are finished. Similar products, equally suitable for detailed masking, are also available from 3M in automotive paint stores.

Finish masking with a combination of regular masking tape and newspaper. Carefully seal all openings in the body, as any paint overspray is hard to remove and easily finds its way past small openings.

Fig. 8-7. Airbrush the yellow base coat using a mixture of Model Master Bright Yellow enamel.

When you have finished masking, seal the edges to prevent bleed-under of the color. Do this by mixing some clear gloss, thinned to the consistency of milk, and applying it to the edges of the masking material with your airbrush. Be careful to avoid spraying too much paint or causing a run.

Why go through this step? Because if there are any tiny gaps in the masking, any paint that does bleed under is clear, and thus invisible. This trick is used by professionals and is good insurance. Figure 8-5 shows the body masked, and fig. 8-6 shows the masked body with the clear paint added.

You are now ready to paint the upper part of the body yellow.

Mix the gloss yellow to the proper consistency, and apply as in previous steps, slowly building it up to a smooth overall gloss. This will take several, sometimes many coats. Be patient! Yellow paint often takes at least several coats to cover a base coat completely.

Don't be tempted to prematurely wet-coat the paint, trying to build up the color intensity. This color just requires more paint to achieve full-depth coverage than most. Make sure the yellow covers the body thoroughly, and don't worry about making it completely glass-smooth on the first coats. Successive coats generally can go on a bit smoother and wetter. This technique takes a bit of practice. It's not a bad idea to test it on an old body surface to become familiar with how the paint sprays and covers.

Once the yellow is complete, let it dry awhile and clean your airbrush. Figure 8-7 shows the body painted in bright yellow. Leave the masking in place, and try to do the next step after you have cleaned the airbrush but before the yellow paint has completely dried.

Step 4: A pearl-yellow overcoat

Next comes a pearl-yellow overcoat over the yellow base coat. You may want to mix this before painting the previous yellow coat on the body. Mix a small amount of pearl powder into prethinned clear gloss (see fig. 8-8); it does not take a lot to achieve the desired effect. Figure 8-9 shows the mixture with the pearl added. Once it's mixed, apply this pearl with your airbrush directly over the yellow, being careful to apply it smoothly over the whole surface.

Fig. 8-8. Mixing the pearl into the paint is easy–just add a pinch of pearl powder to clear enamel.

Fig. 8-9. The clear pearl mixture ready for application. It doesn't take much to get vivid results.

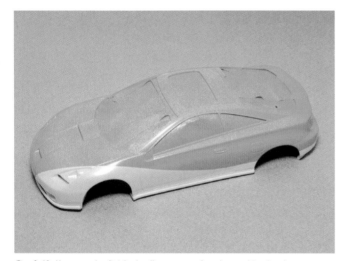

Fig. 8-10. Here are the finished yellow areas, after the masking has been removed.

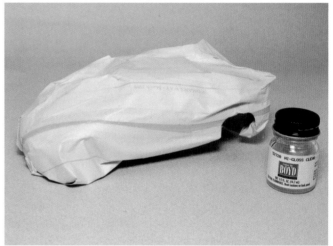

Fig. 8-11. Next step is to mask off the body for the dark blue stripe. Don't forget to spray some clear over the tape edges to prevent color bleed-through.

Cover each panel with the same amount of paint, counting and applying the same number of coats. This is not too difficult. Your painting technique is the same as for previous coats; however, the coat does not have to be super-glossy, just smooth. The surface sheen can be a bit dull, just as long as the finish itself is not grainy.

It takes only a few light coats to achieve the pearl effect. Once this has dried a bit (but not completely), carefully remove the outer masking from the body. The body will look like fig. 8-10 at this point. Let the body dry, and thoroughly clean the airbrush.

Step 5: A contrasting stripe

Next, you will add a darker, contrasting color stripe to the body. As before, mask the body, using your own judgment as to the spacing and width of the stripe. After you've thoroughly masked the surface, add a clear sealer to the area to be painted (see fig. 8-11).

For the stripe, I mixed a dark blue mixture of True Blue Pearl and Copenhagen Blue. Thin this paint, then apply it in the same manner as the previous coats. It builds up rapidly as you spray

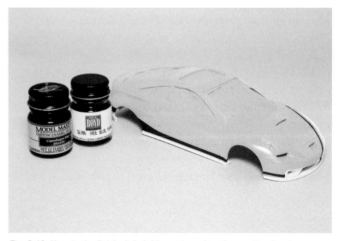

Fig. 8-12. Here is the finished dark blue stripe, after the masking has been removed.

it. After painting, but before the stripe is completely dry, remove the external masking materials. Your body should look like fig. 8-12.

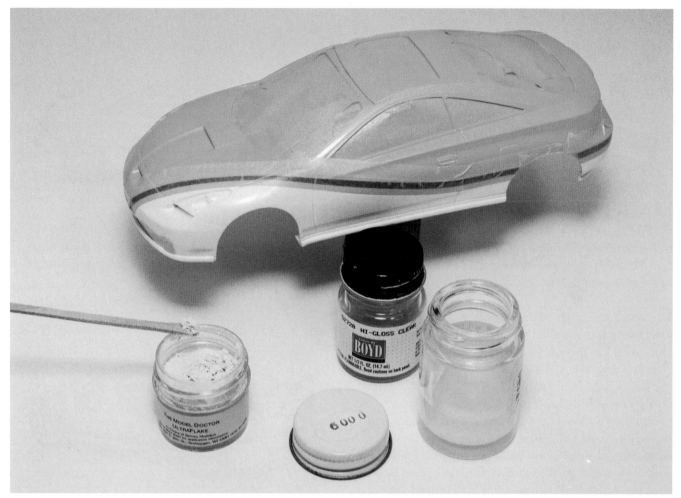

Fig. 8-13. The lower portion of the body, ready for pearly white paint. Add a pinch of pearl powder to some clear; it will cover rapidly with your airbrush.

Fig. 8-14. The painting is almost complete, as seen in this in-progress mockup (with the kit chassis in place).

Fig. 8-15. Add a few carbon fiber decals, and then coat the entire body with clear enamel.

Step 6: Overcoats

You're ready to paint the lower portion of the body with a pearl white overcoat. Mix a small amount of pearl white powder into the prethinned clear. Again, mask all areas of the body that will not be covered in pearl white, leaving just the white base coat area exposed (see fig. 8-13). Also, have another bottle of clear gloss mixed with thinner ready (to clear-coat the entire body

after you have applied the pearl white). If you are concerned that a yellowish tint which may be visible in your clear gloss will adversely affect the clean white color of your model, you can add a few drops of clear blue paint to the clear mixture; this will offset any yellow tint and balance the color.

But don't worry about a very slight tint to the clear; it rarely is visible on a finished model, since the coats are so thin. You

Fig. 8-16. Match the interior color to the color of the carbon fiber decals. I added custom decals to the seats and then sprayed the interior in Testors Dullcote for the proper flat sheen.

Figs. 8-17 to 8-20. The Celica shows off its custom paint job proudly. Already a sleek car, the Celica really acquires some pony-car pizzazz with a few custom details and a high-powered paint job.

Fig. 8-18

may notice that some bottles of clear paint are much more transparent than others. You may want to test various brands of clear paint. Just try them out over your base coats to be sure they are compatible and don't cause the paint underneath to crack or "lift."

Apply the pearl white as in previous steps, then remove the masking, and add several coats of clear gloss to the body. Again, begin slow, making successive coats wetter. You want to apply a good coat of clear without obliterating engraved detail. You want enough clear paint so that you can buff only clear paint when you're polishing the model. The finished body with clear coat is shown in figs. 8-14 and 8-15.

After the clear has dried, you can add other paint and decal details to the body.

Step 7: The interior

Mix the interior color to match the color of carbon-fiber decals on the exterior. I painted the interior a flat dark brown mixed with black.

I then added seat decals for extra detail. To make the surface gloss of these decals match the finish of the flat interior colors, tone them down. Airbrush a mixture of Dullcote clear enamel over the decals and the rest of the interior (see fig. 8-16). This gives a convincing appearance of automotive upholstery. The decals are too glossy to replicate upholstery without this Dullcote finish.

Use your imagination

At this point, you're on your own! Polish the body and add all assembly and finishing details to the model. The finished model looks sharp. The techniques you've acquired can be used for any custom or street-rod project you can imagine. These masking and painting techniques are relatively simple.

As you gain experience, your imagination is the only limiting factor. You can use an airbrush for all sorts of custom painting techniques: flames, scallops, or multicolored effects like murals or the patterns commonly seen on lowriders or street rods.

Let your imagination run wild, use the proper tools and techniques, and your models will reflect your own personal designs.

Fig. 8-19

Fig. 8-20. Don't let those Mustang emblems fool you.

9

Guzzi V10 Centauro

How to Achieve a Spectacular "Showroom" Finish

To really show off your talent with an airbrush, try building a modern motorcycle model. It's an exciting chance to build a model that showcases almost every possible finish. Whether you build a full-blown "crotch-rocket" or a chrome-laden, laid-back cruiser, your airbrush and your creativity are the tools that will bring the colors and finishes alive.

The subject for this project is Tamiya's 1/12 scale Moto Guzzi V10 Centauro kit. This model is a beautiful representation of one of the world's most interesting "standard" motorcycles. In a nutshell, a standard is a fairly simple motorcycle, bridging the gap between sport bikes and cruisers; the rider sits upright and the engine is exposed. This open arrangement allows full visibility of the engine, drive train, and all details of the motorcycle.

I could vividly recall seeing this kit built by a friend a couple of years back. This particular kit has very modern—some might say controversial—styling and would allow me to use a variety of airbrushing effects to help detail the model. The model also has a fair amount of chrome. I knew the combination of gleaming chrome and airbrushed finishes would result in a spectacular shelf model. After a quick trip to the local motorcycle dealership for reference pictures, I was eager to begin.

Model Master Silver Chrome Trim enamel

Model Master Clear Gloss

Gold enamel

Tamiya Gloss Black

Tamiya Semigloss Black

Tamiya Flat Black

Tamiya Clear Orange

Testors Stainless Steel Buffing Metalizer

Testors Aluminum Plate Buffing Metalizer

Testors Gunmetal Buffing Metalizer

Testors Magnesium Buffing Metalizer

Testors Metalizer Sealer

Testors Transparent Blue

Testors Transparent Green

Masking tape

Burnishing tool or toothpick

Hobby knife, no. 11 blade

Fig. 9-1. Airbrush these parts and subassemblies with Model Master Gunmetal Metalizer.

Step 1: Getting started

There are a lot of parts to be painted in a number of colors and finishes. To begin, select the colors and paints you'll use. Take a thorough look through the kit instructions to familiarize yourself with all of the parts and the assembly sequence. This kit has excellent instructions and color references.

You will follow the basic steps of the assembly instructions; however, some of the parts will be assembled and painted as subassemblies, rather than one at a time. This may sound more difficult than it is. Step by step, it is easy to accomplish the painting and assembly of this kit in a reasonable amount of time. (It took me about 20 hours total time to build and detail the Centauro.)

Starting with the engine, put together the subassemblies, preparing all the separate parts to be done in the same color (see fig. 9-1), and paint them with the Gunmetal Buffing Metalizer. Then coat these parts with the sealer. Painting the Metalizer takes only a few minutes. The Testors line of Metalizers is easy to use; they require no thinning, and the colors are so dense they cover almost immediately. You can spray them with just about any type of airbrush; in fact they work quite well with the simplest single-action, external-mix airbrushes.

I painted the parts shown here with a general-purpose "medium" head and cleaned the airbrush with standard lacquer thinner after spraying each Metalizer color. The colors go on so well and so thinly that you lose none of the details underneath. Make sure the part you are painting is smooth, carefully polishing out any parting lines—the Metalizers will not fill any sanding marks or surface defects.

Another nice feature of these colors is that they dry almost immediately.

Step 2: Chrome exhaust system

On most Moto Guzzis, the exhaust system is finished in chrome. The chrome plating in the Centauro kit is excellent, showing few mold lines and a smooth finish. However, on a real bike, the chrome exhaust doesn't remain chrome for more than a few seconds. The heat from combustion discolors the chrome finish, starting at the exhaust flange area next to the cylinder head, and progressively fading out the farther back you go on the pipes. By the time you reach the muffler, the chrome finish is pretty well intact and original.

Basically, if you want a fictitious bike, you can leave the chrome as it is from the kit. If you want it to look realistic, you must weather the pipes.

This is quite easy, using Tamiya Clear Orange airbrushed onto the pipes. Prepare the exhaust pipes, temporarily assembling them to the muffler with either a tiny amount of glue or poster tack, and then mix the Clear Orange with the Tamiya thinner as you would normally, adding anywhere from 10 to 30 percent thinner.

With an airbrush and a regular or medium nozzle, lightly apply a mist of the Clear Orange, starting at the top, where the pipes meet the cylinder heads. Go slowly at first, making sure you don't overdo the application all at once. If you are using a dual-action airbrush, try to spray the paint with a ratio of more air to less paint flow, as far as possible.

Work your way down towards the mufflers; by the time you get to them you should be barely fogging on any paint. Be patient. You want the paint to go on smoothly without running.

Don't worry if the pipes get more color than you expect near the top. If the pipes dry a bit foggy, cover them with a little

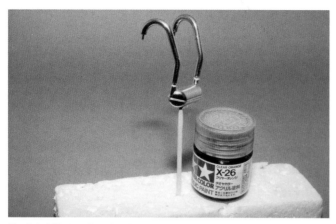

Fig. 9-2. Add minor heat discoloration onto the chrome exhaust by airbrushing Tamiya Clear Orange over the parts until you achieve the desired color.

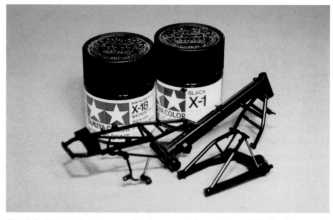

Fig. 9-3. Airbrush the frame and swing arm with a mixture of Tamiya Gloss and Semigloss Black paints for the desired "factory" sheen.

Tamiya Clear Gloss. Set the pipes aside to dry, and they are ready for assembly (see fig. 9-2).

This technique gives the effect of a fairly new bike. You can also add more "bluing" and discoloration over the airbrushed areas later. Common artist's markers (such as the Prismamarkers brand) work well for the effect. You can test the colors at an art supply store. Warm grays and blues work especially well. A good idea is to practice this technique on some of the chrome sprue that comes with the kit, or any from your parts box. Take a look at a real motorcycle for reference, take some notes, and have fun!

Step 3: Chassis and subframe

The chassis and rear swing-arm subframe are next, to be painted in an almost full-gloss black. You can achieve good results with either gloss black or semigloss black alone; however, to me, the finish looked somewhere in between—an easy fix with an airbrush.

As seen in fig. 9-3, mix equal parts of Tamiya Gloss Black and Semigloss Black. Thin the paint with Tamiya thinner, and make a few practice runs on an old body or piece of cardboard to familiarize yourself with the paint flow. If the paint is mixed correctly, it will flow very smoothly from the airbrush.

Do the basic assembly, clean up parting lines, and apply the black paint mixture on the parts (with a high-flow nozzle, if possible). The black covers quickly. You may find that it goes on rather wet. You can help dry the parts between coats by using the air flow from your airbrush without any paint.

Once a few coats have been applied, subsequent paint coats cover even better. These paints dry rather quickly, especially if you use a dehydrator to accelerate drying time.

Step 4: Various parts

Next, you will airbrush the various chassis detail parts. First, detail the brake rotors. Start by cleaning the parts, mount them for painting, and mix some Testors Gold with some Clear gloss enamel.

You'll want to use about a 30:70 ratio of gold to clear. Be careful not to mix too much; you're painting just a couple of small items, and the exact ratio is not that important. Thin this mixture roughly 50:50 with Testors enamel thinner for airbrushing, and paint the rotors (see fig. 9-4).

The paint covers quickly; once it's applied, put the parts aside to dry overnight. Again, a dehydrator will cut the drying time if you are impatient.

Fig. 9-4. First spray the brake rotors with a mixture of Testors Gold and Clear for the desired sheen.

Fig. 9-5. Then, once the gold paint is dry, mask it as shown.

Fig. 9-6. Airbrush Model Master Stainless Steel Buffing Metalizer onto the brake rotors. When dry, buff them to simulate the bright contact surface of the rotors.

Fig. 9-7. Use two shades of Model Master metalizers on the fork tubes–Aluminum Plate and Magnesium. Seal both with metalizer sealer.

The next step is to mask the center of the rotors, which will remain gold (see fig. 9-5), and paint the outer portions of the rotors with Stainless Steel Buffing Metalizer. Afterwards, let the metalizer dry, then buff the finish with a cotton swab (see fig. 9-6). This gives a very convincing appearance to the brake rotors, especially if you apply a black wash with a brush to the surfaces of the rotors to highlight the drilled details.

The fork tubes are next, to be painted in two colors: Testors Magnesium and Aluminum Plate Buffing Metalizers. Paint the upper portions in Magnesium and the lower portions in Aluminum Plate (see fig. 9-7). As these colors are not to be buffed, you must use sealer over the metalizers. This will allow you to mask over them without removing any of the metallic finish. Again, these paints cover and dry rapidly, and match the factory finish nicely.

Finally, paint the rest of the ancillary chassis components in Aluminum Plate Metalizer. Clean, mount, and spray all parts with the Aluminum Plate, and then seal them (see fig. 9-8), and leave them to dry. The actual time spent painting is a fraction of the time you'll spend cleaning each part and mounting them to the fixture for airbrushing. But this time is well spent; it will yield the most realistic-looking results.

Fig. 9-8. Spray these chassis components with Aluminum Plate Metalizer and then seal them.

Fig. 9-9. Airbrush these plastic and metal detail components with Tamiya Semigloss Black for a realistic surface sheen.

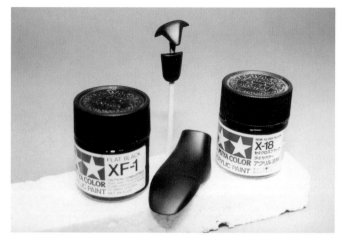
Fig. 9-10. Simulate the vinyl texture on the seat and tank padding by spraying an unthinned mixture of Tamiya Semigloss and Flat Black paints.

Step 5: Semigloss Black components

Next up are various plastic and metal components on the motorcycle, all to be painted in Semigloss Black (see fig. 9-9). Clean all parts and prepare, mount, and spray them with Tamiya Semigloss Black, thinned accordingly. Some of the kit parts are molded in black, some in silver. The black ones are the easiest to cover.

If your airbrush has a high-flow tip, use it for these acrylics; it will help the paint flow best and achieve the proper finish. If you are using a dual-action airbrush to spray acrylics, often it is best to start slowly with a ratio of more air to less paint flow. This helps the initial coats adhere well to the plastic. After applying a few coats, you can add more paint to the flow and less air. Practice yields the best results.

Step 6: Vinyl parts

The final detail components you'll airbrush are the vinyl parts: the seat and the fuel tank pads. These parts are molded in black and look best with a pebble-grained finish that simulates vinyl. I used a combination of Tamiya Semigloss and Flat Blacks and mixed them with a smaller amount of thinner than usual. By varying the pressure and the consistency of the paint with your airbrush, you can achieve a remarkable variety of finishes.

Practice spraying this mixture a few times, and then paint the parts. By carefully manipulating the air pressure and the distance from which you spray, you can get a nice, pebble-grained finish on your vinyl parts (see fig. 9-10).

If you are using a dual-action airbrush, you can spray air over the parts to help dry them. You can also manipulate the paint flow to apply just a minuscule splattering of paint to the surface. (This technique also works very well to simulate a vinyl roof on an automobile.) What you end up with are parts that look soft to the touch, just like vinyl. You may even be able to spray these acrylics without thinner for this step.

Step 7: Painting in Gloss Silver

The body of the Moto Guzzi from the factory is two-tone in color. In this project, I wanted to show a couple of techniques that work well for painting automobile and motorcycle models alike. The motorcycle has silver-painted side covers and wheels; you'll have to paint them in Gloss Silver. Also, I wanted to render the rest of the body in a candy color, to simulate a factory finish, but with a touch of "custom" effect that looks like a factory-applied custom color.

Therefore, you'll paint all of the body components Gloss Silver—as a base coat for the candy color, and the finished color for other parts.

Start by preassembling and cleaning up all of the parts. I used gap-filling super glue on the tank. You can also use liquid styrene cement to weld the pieces together; just make sure they dry thoroughly before painting—or a seam may appear later. Luckily, much of the seam on this model is covered by padding and the rear seat cowl.

The next step is the most important to achieve a beautiful, in-scale, Gloss Silver paint finish. Mix Testors Model Master Silver Chrome Trim enamel with Clear Gloss (about $\frac{1}{3}$ silver and about $\frac{2}{3}$ clear). Thin this mixture about 50:50 with thinner, to a milky consistency. Spray this mixture on the parts. It will build up rapidly. You do not have to be too careful to make this coat very wet or glossy. Just misting the color on may give you the best metallic finish, depending on the consistency and airflow.

Once the silver is in place, cover it with a clear coat finish, using Clear Gloss thinned roughly 50:50 with thinner.

Figure 9-11 shows all of the parts painted in Gloss Silver. Put them aside to dry, especially the main body, which you will mask in the next step.

Fig. 9-11. Some components are Gloss Silver, while some will have a transparent "candy" color. Their basecoat is an airbrushed mixture of Model Master Silver Chrome Trim and Clear for the correct gloss silver finish.

Fig. 9-12. Use cans of Testors Transparent Blue and Candy Emerald Green for the airbrushed color coats on the fenders and tank. Spray the colors into a glass jar first, then transfer and spray the mixture through your airbrush.

Step 8: Candy colors

"Candy" colors, which are basically transparent colors applied over a reflective metallic base coat, are quite vivid and popular on both motorcycles and custom cars. They can also be tricky to deal with, so you must be very careful applying these colors to your models.

But properly executed, the candies will be so glossy, and the color so deep, that you may not even need to clear coat or to polish them.

Paint them with a high-flow nozzle if possible, although a general-purpose nozzle is sufficient. You'll have to be vigilant while painting to cover all parts with the right amount of paint and at the correct angle.

If you don't spray evenly, you will develop lines, or "stripes," in your paint. And if you spray on too much paint at one time, it will cause the paint to pull away from edges. Too much paint in one area will result in a blotchy appearance.

So practice passing the airbrush over the model in smooth, even strokes, covering the entire surface with a uniform thickness of paint.

Start by masking the tank areas that will remain silver. Next, take spray cans of Transparent Blue and Transparent Green, and spray them directly into one of your airbrush jars. The reason I used spray cans of this paint is simple: it's the only way (I know of) to get compatible, clear-colored, enamel tints. And they happen to be prethinned, and work well through the airbrush.

Use equal parts blue and green, and apply them in a number of light coats to the body, front fender, and seat cowl (see fig. 9-12). As you paint, count the number of coats on the body, and carefully match the number of coats to the other parts, so the colors will appear equal.

Spray the coats on lightly at first. By the final coat, you should use the maximum flow of air and paint through the airbrush. Afterwards, let the parts dry, and remove the masking once the body is dry enough to handle (but before it is completely dry, if possible). Twenty to 30 minutes should be sufficient.

Step 9: Final assembly and detailing

All the subassemblies are now painted. From here, assembling and detailing the finished model will come together quickly. Following kit directions, complete your assembly step-by-step, and you will see the rewards of your airbrushed paint finishes immediately.

Fig. 9-13. The completed model looks quite sharp in its finished paints, giving a high level of detail to a completely "out-of-the-box" buildup.

A Pleasure to the eye

The realism of the model is enhanced by the finishes you use to complete it (see fig. 9-13). Following these steps, you have used your airbrush in most of the ways you need to achieve show-quality paint finishes.

Even built out of the box with no aftermarket details, you have created an impressive model with a lot of detail to please the eye. The same techniques can be used for full-fairing racing bikes—or custom choppers. The painting techniques and varied finishes really make this a fun model to build.

Once you have finished just one motorcycle, you will proba-bly be inspired to build many others.

10

'68 Dodge Charger

Step-by-Step Techniques to Achieve a Convincing "Factory" Finish

This chapter will show you how to create a paint finish with an airbrush on a rather complex project. The steps will help you learn a wide range of techniques for detailing a model. The project here is a Revell 1968 Dodge Charger. To make this car, I'll combine parts from two models: Revell's 1969 Dodge Charger and Revell's 1968 Dick Landy Dodge Charger.

To achieve my goal—building the 1968 Charger stock—I have to combine the two kits (along with a stock air cleaner and decal from a parts-box '67 Plymouth GTX).

The 1968 Charger kit has no vinyl top, while the 1969 kit does. But the molded vinyl top on the '69 Charger is a bit out of scale. And a technique I use for simulating vinyl will work better on the smooth roof.

Also, per kit instructions, I revised the side marker lamps to their 1968 configuration. For this, you'll need to fill the rectangular lenses on the body and either use the kit-supplied round marker lights or (as I did) add thin slices of Evergreen styrene tubing to replicate those side markers.

Testors Model Master Gray Primer

Boyd White Primer

Testors Model Master Chrome Yellow

Testors Model Master French Blue

Model Master Flat Black

Boyd True Blue Pearl

Model Master Copenhagen Blue

Model Master Silver Chrome Trim

Boyd High Gloss Clear

Boyd High Gloss White

Testors Airbrush Thinner

Tamiya (or similar) masking tape

Bare Metal Foil

Tamiya Semigloss Black Acrylic

Tamiya Flat Black Acrylic

MCW Light Gray Primer

MCW Hemi Orange Metallic

Metalizer Burnt Metal Buffing Metalizer

Metalizer Aluminum Plate Buffing Metalizer

Metalizer Burnt Iron Buffing Metalizer

Metalizer Sealer

Wide masking tape

Newspaper for masking

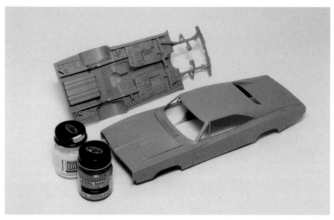

Fig. 10-1. All 1968 Chargers were painted with a light gray primer underneath their final color coats. Testors Model Master Gray Primer and Boyd White Primer can be mixed to replicate the shade of light gray primer used on the real car.

Step 1: Priming

Begin by performing all necessary body work. Besides cleaning up and removing mold lines, I added some .040 Evergreen half-round to the base of the roof for the vinyl roof chrome trim, and as mentioned above, I added tiny slices of styrene tubing to simulate side markers.

The model will be primed in light gray. The center of the chassis is to be left in the primer color, and since Model Master Gray Primer is slightly darker than the shade I wanted, I mixed some Boyd White Primer to the gray primer to lighten it (to replicate the light gray used by Dodge).

Mix the two primers 50:50, then add about 50 percent thinner. Using either a medium- or high-flow nozzle, begin spraying the model. Start with a light mist coat over all surfaces, holding the airbrush perpendicular to the surface you are spraying. The primer will cover quickly, in just a few coats. Your final coats can be sprayed a bit heavier and glossier.

Put the parts aside to dry. When they're dry, inspect them for any imperfections. If you find any dust or rough areas, sand them carefully, preferably with a polishing cloth. Once they're smooth, recoat the primer until the color is uniform, and let dry (see fig. 10-1).

Step 2: A solid basecoat

We will replicate an actual color used on the '68 Charger: Medium Blue Iridescent. Based on an original color chip, we can mix hobby enamels to match this. However, hobby enamels, in metallic form, generally have pigments that do not build up quickly. They tend to have a lot of clear, and if you try to spray them, you may become frustrated by the amount of time and paint it takes to get a saturated color.

To alleviate this problem, I use a solid color basecoat underneath hobby enamel metallics. This allows me to get color saturation quickly, so there is less paint on the model, and engraved details still show through.

The solid-color basecoat is easy to mix. It does not have to be an exact match—just close. I chose Model Master French Blue, mixed with a few drops of Chrome Yellow, and mixed that 50:50 with the light gray mixture I used previously. Thinned to the consistency of milk, this color is close to the final color and covers very well, giving the model a smooth, semigloss basecoat.

With your medium- or high-flow nozzle, apply this mixture as you did the primer, in a preliminary light coat, adding a couple of coats on top of that until the color is uniform over all of the parts. Figure 10-2 shows the body and chassis finished in the basecoat.

Let the parts dry, then check for imperfections. If there are any dust particles, polish them out and if needed, add another coat of the basecoat. It is important that this basecoat is very uniform in color; it will affect the metallic colors applied over it. Especially important is the hood. Make sure that it matches at this point. If not, it may never match!

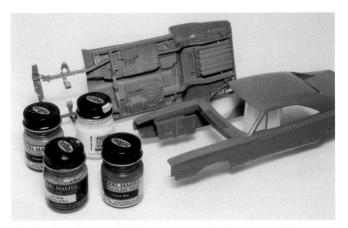

Fig. 10-2. To replicate the 1968 Charger Medium Blue Iridescent paint in enamels, begin with a solid-color basecoat that is similar to the final color. To create this result, add a mixture of Model Master French Blue and a few drops of Chrome Yellow to the gray/white primer mixture (from the previous step) for the basecoat, and spray it onto the model in several coats.

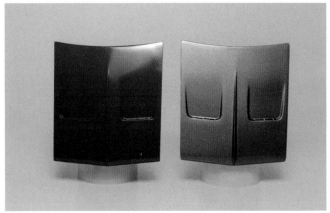

Fig. 10-3. These hoods provide a good comparison between the solid basecoat color and the final Medium Blue Iridescent. A basecoat should be similar to the final color, but it does not have to be exactly the same. With a color-matched basecoat, you can spray metallic colors (which tend to have significantly less pigment) in fewer coats, allowing fine details to show through.

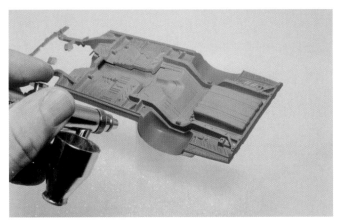

Fig. 10-4. Chrysler products from the late '60s generally have a chassis whose visible colors are a mixture of primer at the center and oversprayed color coats from the front, sides, and rear of the car. This is easy to replicate by spraying the base and color coats at about a 45-degree angle from the sides (as seen here), applying the color only near the edges, leaving the center section in uncovered primer.

Fig. 10-5. If possible, try to find a genuine factory color chip to help you match the original color accurately. Authentic, original color chips can be found at some automotive paint stores for newer cars and at swap meets and specialized vendors for older cars.

Once the underhood area is basecoated and dried, it may be helpful to install the hood and paint it at the same time as the front fenders, so they have the same amount of paint and color saturation. Figure 10-3 shows the hood in basecoat next to a finished hood.

Figure 10-4 shows the chassis being painted with the basecoat. The chassis paint is fogged to replicate the actual car as delivered from the factory. Notice that there is very little blue paint in the center; only the sides and perimeter of the chassis are covered by overspray from the body being painted. This is an easy effect to achieve with your airbrush: just spray the color lightly around the edges of the chassis, at roughly a 45-degree angle. Adjust your spray pressure and lightly apply the paint for the proper effect; it will take only few minutes.

Step 3: Mixing the metallic blue

To match the color chip, you will use mostly Boyd True Blue Pearl, with a little Silver Chrome Trim for a bit of brightness and for fine metallic particles, and a little Copenhagen Blue to darken the color slightly (see fig. 10-5). The exact ratio of colors is not crucial, as the True Blue Pearl is very close to the proper color.

In a paint jar, mix roughly 10 parts True Blue to 1 part Copenhagen Blue, plus just a few drops of Silver Chrome Trim. Be careful with the silver. Add just a few drops at a time, as it lightens the color rapidly. If you add too much, it takes a lot of the blue colors to re-adjust.

Stir the colors until you are satisfied with the match. With a toothpick and a piece of white cardboard or styrene as a palette, compare your color with the chip. You will need to mix at least

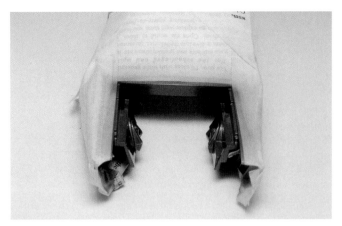

Fig. 10-6. To paint the hood exactly the same color as the rest of the car, it must be in place when the body is painted. So mask and paint the underhood area, which also must be the same color, before the rest of the body. You can also paint the underside of the hood at the same time. This process helps avoid a common problem: the hood ends up noticeably lighter or darker than the rest of the model. Planning ahead helps to avoid such last-minute problems, which affect the quality of your model's finish.

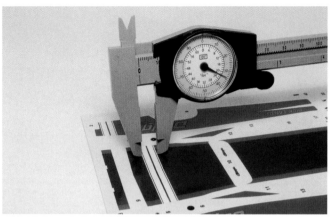

Fig. 10-7. To replicate the kit's "bumblebee" stripe decal in another color, using paint, start by measuring the decal. Dial calipers seen here work well for checking the exact dimensions of line width and spacing. If you are working only from photographs, you either need to do background research on the exact measurements—or make a calculated guess and create something that looks good to you and seems to match the photographs.

Fig. 10-8. Using photos or decals as reference, thoroughly mask the stripe area to be painted with a combination of Bare Metal Foil and Tamiya or similar brands of masking tape. To ensure none of the stripe color bleeds through, first spray a coat of clear over the masks. Any paint that does bleed through will be clear, nearly invisible, and easily polished smooth.

Fig. 10-9. Use Model Master flat black enamel to rapidly apply very thin, light coats of opaque black to the stripe area of the model. You can use flat black, since you will later clear-coat the entire body for a final gloss. You may use gloss black at this point if you wish; however, flat black tends to cover better with fewer coats.

a half-ounce of the metallic blue, and you might want a bit more to practice with. Mix it with thinner to the consistency of milk, and you are ready to start painting the metallic blue.

Step 4: Applying the blue

I used a medium tip to spray the metallic color. It gives a smoother flow to the metallic particles, making them appear more in scale. Because I will use a clear topcoat, I must apply the metallic color smoothly, but it does not have to be very glossy and can have a little grain to the finish. As long as it does not have a lot of "orange peel" effect or dust, a slightly dull appearance is fine.

I covered the model in the metallic blue in the same way as the primer coats: a light coat to start, and several heavier coats to build up the color.

I installed the hood before painting the metallic blue. This ensures an exact color match but requires another step. Once the body is dry, I masked the underhood area to spray the same metallic color over the basecoat (see fig. 10-6). Also, don't forget to paint the underside of the hood itself. The metallic mixture covers quite well; the Silver Chrome Trim paint makes the mixture a bit more opaque. And don't forget to mist a few coats on the edges of the chassis!

Clean the airbrush thoroughly.

Fig. 10-10. Preplanning and careful application of masking materials and paint result in a crisp, accurate paint stripe. The body is now ready for the final clear gloss coats.

Fig. 10-11. Using photo references or another model to duplicate, carefully measure, cut, and apply a center mask for the vinyl top. Make sure the lines of the mask are parallel and centered on the roof. You can replicate the overlapping seams visible on a vinyl roof by overlapping the clear gloss coats in two steps. In the first step, mask the center of the roof, then coat the entire body with several coats of clear. Make sure to apply the final clear coats liberally, especially onto the roof area. This will give the seams added depth.

Step 5: The bumblebee stripe

Once the metallic blue is dry and you have polished out and recoated any imperfections, you are ready to add the rear "bumblebee" stripe. I used photographs as reference and used the kit decals to figure out the exact size. Figure 10-7 shows measurements taken directly from the kit decals.

Start masking the stripe by adding tape to the outside edges of the stripe area. Then cut thin strips of Bare Metal Foil and apply them to the center portion of the stripe area (see fig. 10-8). Once burnished down, the stripe masking will be covered by a light coat of clear to seal the edges. Mix the clear (as most enamels) to the consistency of milk, and spray it lightly to a sheen. If any paint does seep under the masking, it is clear and invisible.

Once the clear has set, mix some flat black enamel for the stripe. Apply it as you did the clear, in several light coats. The flat black covers quickly, so you need not add much paint to the surface. The paint should be smooth, with a uniform dull appearance, which will be covered by clear gloss. Figure 10-9 shows the flat black as applied. This step takes only takes a few minutes. Remember to clean the airbrush thoroughly you're when done.

Once the stripe has dried a while, but not completely—about 30 minutes—remove the masking material. Figure 10-10 shows a perfectly executed stripe. It's easy if you follow the steps above.

Step 6: A first clear coat

You are ready to apply a clear coat to the body. This is done in two steps. That way, the thickness of the clear coat on the roof will make the overlapping seams visible on the vinyl top.

Begin by measuring the desired width of the center section of the vinyl top. You will mask this area for the application of the first coats of clear gloss (see fig. 10-11). I used the extra '69 body for the measurement, or you can use photographs or your own eye for the proper proportion.

Apply the clear gloss with a high-flow nozzle if possible. Mix it to a milky consistency, or even slightly thinner. If too thick, it will show too much grain or orange peel; too thin, and it will not cover well. This is to be the final coat, so be careful to brush or blow off dust or lint on the surface before you spray. Apply the first coat lightly and uniformly over the entire model. You can paint the model with the hood installed, as the underhood area need not be as glossy as the body.

Add subsequent coats, using smooth strokes of your whole arm, perpendicular to the surface, until the paint is smooth. Generally, I use one mist coat, and anywhere from three to five (sometimes more) heavier coats of clear.

The final coat should be done quickly, close to the model but at lightning speed. This gives you tremendous gloss, without adding so much paint that it runs. Practice this technique on a spare body before you do this the first time. It is easy to overdo the paint—or to be too cautious, making your gloss coats a bit grainy because you are afraid to get it too wet. There are fine lines between a grainy finish, a perfect gloss finish . . . and a paint run! Practice this heavy flow on a spare body. You must move your arm very quickly back and forth above the surface of the model to apply the paint. Once you've perfected the technique, you will get amazing gloss on your final coats—with no paint runs.

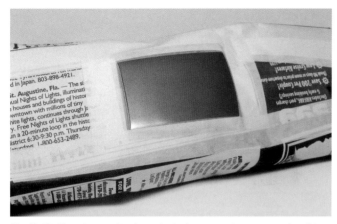

Fig. 10-12. After clear-coating the entire body, remove the center mask and let the clear coat dry thoroughly. Then, remask the body to add the overlapping center section of the vinyl top (as seen here). Paint the center section liberally with the same clear gloss mixture. When it has dried for about 30 minutes, you can carefully remove the masking.

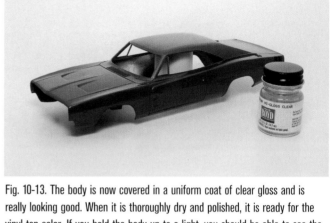

Fig. 10-13. The body is now covered in a uniform coat of clear gloss and is really looking good. When it is thoroughly dry and polished, it is ready for the vinyl top color. If you hold the body up to a light, you should be able to see the overlapping vinyl top, ready to paint.

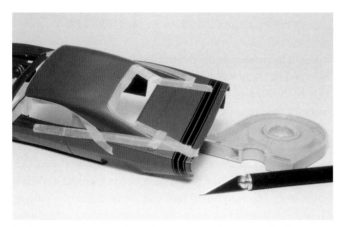

Fig. 10-14. Careful masking is needed to paint the vinyl top over the finished color coat underneath. Add the masking tape, burnish it, and use a fresh no. 11 blade to trim the edges accurately. Make sure the top area is clean of any fingerprints or polishing residue to avoid any potential problems with the vinyl top color. It's a good idea at this point to seal the edges with clear (as you did earlier with the bumblebee stripe, see fig. 10-8) to avoid color bleed-through.

Fig. 10-15. Spray equal parts Tamiya Flat Black and Semigloss Black without thinner onto the roof. This will give you a nice, in-scale texture that accurately represents a vinyl top. Use a test card to practice spraying the texture seen here, before actually spraying your model. When you are comfortable with the texture and spray pattern, you are ready to paint the model.

Step 7: A second clear coat

Once you have applied the first clear coat, let it dry and then mask it (see fig. 10-12) to add another layer to replicate the center of the vinyl top. Be sure to mask the edges of the center section, leaving about ¹⁄₃₂″ of the previous clear layer exposed. This is the visible overlap of the vinyl sections; it will show through the next step, painting the roof itself. You can see the faint line of the previous clear coat in the photograph, near the bottom edge of the masking. After masking the top, apply several coats of clear to the top, let it dry slightly, and remove the masking material. Clean the airbrush. Figure 10-13 shows the body in finished clear.

Step 8: Painting the vinyl top

Our next step is to paint the vinyl top. Begin by masking the chrome edges surrounding the top (see fig. 10-14). Once the fine masking is done, finish masking the entire body with wide masking tape and newspaper (see fig. 10-15).

Mix up equal parts of Tamiya Flat Black and Semigloss Black acrylics. You do not need more than about ¼ ounce. You will want to spray this unthinned if possible—to intentionally achieve a pebble-grain effect. Set your airbrush pressure as low as possible to spray this paint. (The practice card in fig. 10-15 shows the low-pressure spray pattern.)

Apply this pebbly-thick paint to the top slowly; it will cover quickly. Practice with the air pressure, and add small amounts of thinner only if necessary to allow the paint to flow from the airbrush. You may want to use the gravity-feed open cup on the airbrush if you have one; the thicker acrylic seems to flow better from it.

Fig. 10-16. The Charger's body paint is now finished. The black stripe and the vinyl top are a good complement to the medium metallic-blue body. Careful attention to color, detail, and application will reward you with models that look like miniature versions of the real thing, not merely "models."

Fig. 10-17. The Charger's engine is Hemi Orange. MCW Automotive Finishes makes the exact color (it is actually a metallic). To paint the motor, first build the subassembly of all parts to be painted in Hemi Orange. Then prime the parts and finally paint them with Hemi Orange.

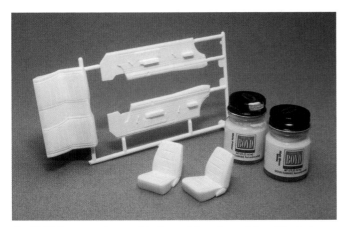

Fig. 10-18. To represent accurately the semigloss sheen of the white vinyl material on the Charger's seats and door panels, use a mixture of Boyd White Primer and High Gloss White enamels. You can spray them on without a coat of primer.

Step 9: The engine

Now it's time to turn your attention to painting the details on the rest of the kit components. The Hemi engine from the kit is trimmed, cleaned, and assembled. To the assembly, I applied a coat of MCW light gray primer. This paint is prethinned and generally does not require any thinner. Use a high-flow nozzle if possible, and be careful to get all the various surfaces, nooks, and crannies covered. The airbrush allows you to take special care. It does not spray a large volume of paint, as a spray can would, and allows all the fine details to show through.

After the primer is dry, apply a few coats of MCW Hemi Orange metallic to the engine. It has a very slight metallic effect and in this scale looks very accurate. Apply it as the other coats: start light and build up slowly, covering all details carefully then using a final wet coat for gloss. Figure 10-17 shows the engine and paints used. The painting process took less than an hour, including drying time between applying the primer and the Hemi Orange.

Step 10: The interior

The interior color I've used is white, with black carpet and dashboard, common on late '60s automobiles. It shows off interior detailing nicely on a model. The front seats were assembled and the rear seat was attached to the door panel section of sprue (see fig. 10-18). The white paint I chose to replicate the vinyl is a simple mixture of Boyd White Primer and High Gloss White, about a 50:50 mixture.

I thinned it appropriately and sprayed it onto the seats and door panels in several light coats, until the color was uniform and the seams on the front seats were invisible. Spray these parts lightly; too much paint can fill in fine details, and you don't want the final color to show more than a slight amount of gloss.

Once a uniform color has been built up on the top, you may want to add a small amount of thinner to the black mixture and apply a few light coats over the previous ones to ensure a good, solid coat of black.

Clean the airbrush thoroughly. The acrylic dries rapidly, so in only a few minutes, you can remove the masking to reveal the finished vinyl roof (see fig. 10-16). The effect is amazing: a very nice, in-scale appearance with far more realistic seams than those engraved in the other kit. This is probably as accurate a vinyl top as you can get on a model, and it can be done in any number of colors.

It also looks good with a light coat of Armor All—just like a real car!

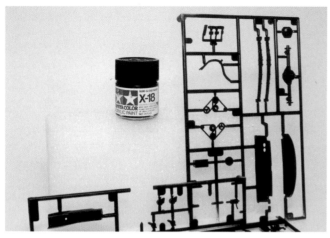

Fig. 10-19. A good number of chassis and engine detail parts are finished in Tamiya Semigloss Black. To speed the paint process, you can spray many of the parts while they're still attached to the sprue. It is easy to touch up parting lines and areas where the parts are clipped from the sprue after painting the entire tree. This is especially true when you're using a black paint. If parts require a lot of trimming or cleanup, you may need to paint them individually, which adds considerable time but gives contest-quality results.

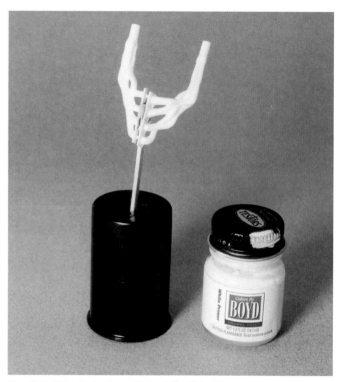

Fig. 10-20. Paint the headers with Boyd Flat White Primer.

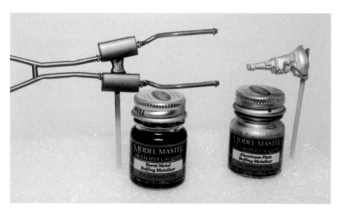

Fig. 10-21. Use Model Master Metalizers to finish the exhaust and transmission. Paint the exhaust in Burnt Metal and the transmission in Aluminum Plate. These colors require no thinner to spray through most airbrushes, and they cover rapidly in very thin coats.

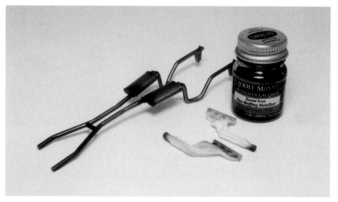

Fig. 10-22. Replicating the burned, weathered appearance commonly seen on exhaust components is easy to do with a light application of Burnt Iron Metalizer using your airbrush. This simple effect gives the components depth and dimension.

Step 11: Additional components

Next, prepare the trees with the model's components that you'll paint satin black (see fig. 10-19). This will save you a good bit of time, compared to either brush-painting or separating the parts before painting. The semigloss is easy to touch up at the attachment points while you're assembling the kit. I airbrushed on a few coats of Tamiya Semigloss Black; I thinned the paint slightly for good flow and rotated the tree while painting each component. Apply this paint as the others: use a fine mist coat to begin, and apply latter coats more heavily.

The valve covers on a Hemi are textured black, so I sprayed unthinned Tamiya Flat Black on the valve covers. I painted the headers in Boyd White Primer (see fig. 10-20).

I used metalizers for details such as the exhaust system and transmission. Figure 10-21 shows the assembled transmission (painted with Aluminum Plate metalizer) and the basic exhaust system (painted with Burnt Metal metalizer). Spray the metalizers directly from the bottle with no thinning. They cover rapidly, taking only a minute or two per component. Seal these parts with Metalizer Sealer.

Fig. 10-23. When all of the kit parts are painted and dry, follow assembly instructions to build the model. The chassis and interior are looking good at this point. Careful painting, assembly, and details combine to reward you with a realistic miniature appearance.

Fig. 10-24. Notice how the components of the chassis really stand out at this point. The carefully layered colors—using your new skills to paint with precision with your airbrush—really give the chassis an authentic look. With all the fine details, this model really looks good.

For a final detail, I added some careful weathering to the exhaust components. Figure 10-22 shows the headers and the exhaust system, detailed with a slight amount of Burnt Iron metalizer. Apply it with a light touch, with as little pressure as possible. Detail each joint in the exhaust this way. It gives a nice realistic appearance.

That's it!

This completes the airbrush techniques for this model. The rest of the assembly involves detailing with a brush, foiling, and applying decals. Figure 10-23 shows the assembled interior and chassis before assembly. Figure 10-24 shows the finished chassis after final assembly to the body. Notice the fogged effects

achieved with the airbrush: the primer/color fogging of the basic chassis and the weathered joints of the exhaust system. If you are brave, you could mix up a very thin mixture of "dirt" and further weather the chassis with the airbrush.

Figure 10-26 (see next page) shows the engine detail as installed; the only aftermarket accessory in this engine compartment is the plug wires. The kit engine is detailed with a stock air cleaner and decal from a '67 GTX.

The final model (see figs. 10-25 and 10-27) really came out well. With good painting techniques and careful detailing and foil application, your models can be just as realistic!

This is a model of a car I have wanted to build for a long time, and I'm happy to show you how to achieve similar results for

Figs. 10-25 to 10-27. The final appearance of this model shows off your attention to fine details, achieved with the help of your airbrush. With the exception of the chrome vinyl top trim, this model was built to box-stock standards. The model truly looks like a miniature of the real car, especially in photographs. These techniques are fairly easy as you gain skill and familiarity with your airbrush.

your models. You may choose to custom-mix your paint as I did, or you could order it from MCW or an automotive paint store. I find it convenient to mix hobby paints that I already have—or can easily purchase from a local hobby shop.

Either way, with your airbrush and good reference photos, you can end up with an impressive replica of your favorite car!

At first glance, it may seem quite a challenge to achieve a final finish like this. But taking one step at a time, you will be able to pull off consistently spectacular finishes on your models—with more accuracy and in less time than you might think.

Fig. 10-26

Fig. 10-27

A Realistic "Raw Metal" Finish Is Not as Hard as It Looks

A raw-metal finish on an aircraft model is a sight to behold—if it is finished properly. Sometimes a model builder pulls off such a feat and successfully replicates the many variations of colors and finishes needed to accomplish this. I'm always impressed when I see a model like this at a show or hobby shop.

Because the builder must paint plastic to replicate unpainted metal, and because many aircraft are made from a number of differing metals, this is one of the most complicated types of paint jobs to accomplish faithfully.

Before tackling this model, I had never tried this type of finish before, but the challenge was enough to make me enthusiastic—and focused on taking the proper steps. If I can be successful, you can too. Plan ahead, think ahead, research the model you are building, and follow step-by-step instructions.

Be prepared to practice any new techniques before trying them on your model. Try them out first on a scrap body or on plain pieces of styrene. Familiarize yourself with the techniques of spraying, polishing, masking, and overcoating the layers, and you can achieve a wonderful variety of metal finishes on your model's surface.

Model Master Aluminum Plate Nonbuffing Metalizer
Model Master Aluminum Plate Buffing Metalizer
Model Master Gunmetal Buffing Metalizer
Model Master Gunmetal Nonbuffing Metalizer
Model Master Dark Anodonic Gray Buffing Metalizer
Model Master Stainless Steel Buffing Metalizer
Boyd White Primer
Testors Dullcote Lacquer
Testors Airbrush Thinner
Lacquer Thinner
AeroMaster Warpac Cockpit Blue Green
AeroMaster Radome/Hub Green
Tamiya Medium Gray
Tamiya Buff
Tamiya Flat Black
Gunze Clear
Gunze FS 36375 Gray
Gunze FS 34092 Dark Green
Gunze Thinner
AeroMaster/Poly S airbrush thinner or bottled or distilled water

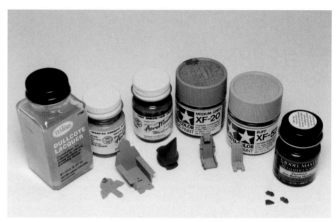

Fig. 11-1. Here you see a variety of cockpit components, with the paints used to airbrush their details.

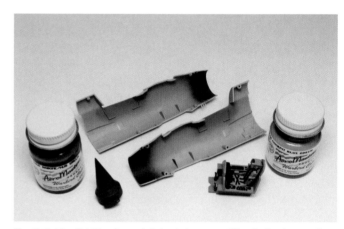

Fig. 11-2. After finishing the cockpit but before assembling the fuselage section, paint the interior cockpit portion of the fuselage in AeroMaster Cockpit Blue Green and the portion around the nosecone Radome/Hub Green.

The model seen here is an excellent subject for either beginners or seasoned modelers. It is a MiG 21 in 1/48 scale, made by Academy. The model is well-engineered, has clear assembly instructions, and assembles without particular problems. The parts fit very well and require only a minimum of filling and finishing prior to painting.

Step 1: Painting the cockpit

Each step of the model assembly shown will follow the kit instructions. The first area to paint is the cockpit (see fig. 11-1). Paint the basic cockpit and instrument panel in AeroMaster Cockpit Blue Green. Trim and clean the parts.

Prepare your airbrush with either a fine or medium tip; test-spray the color through the airbrush to see how it flows. If it needs thinning, add a few drops of either bottled or distilled water or AeroMaster/Poly S thinner to the mixture.

Once it sprays smoothly, apply it to the cockpit and instrument panel. This color will cover rapidly. When you're finished, set the parts aside to dry. At this point, you will also want to paint the inner parts of the fuselage in the same color (see fig. 11-2). Clean the airbrush thoroughly with water or rubbing alcohol.

When the instrument panel has dried, you may want to coat it with a layer of Testors Dullcote Lacquer (if you will be detail-painting the instruments with brush-painted acrylics, as I did). The Dullcote will protect the underlying surface from mixing with the acrylic brush paints. Mix the Dullcote about 50:50 with either lacquer thinner or Model Master Airbrush enamel thinner; apply it to both the instrument panel and cockpit.

Set the parts aside to dry, and clean the airbrush with lacquer thinner. When the instrument panel is dry, you can brush-paint the instrument details as you see fit.

Step 2: The nosecone

The next part to detail is the nosecone. Follow kit instructions on adding lead fishing weights inside the cone. When the glue is dry, you are ready to paint it with AeroMaster Radome/Hub Green.

As before, test-spray the paint to see if it needs thinning. If so, use either bottled water or AeroMaster/Poly S thinner. This color also covers rapidly. When the nosecone is painted, set it aside to dry.

Next, spray the green on the inner surfaces of the fuselage (see fig. 11-2). Afterwards, clean the airbrush with water or rubbing alcohol.

Fig. 11-3. Before assembling the rear section, finish the turbine subassembly and paint the inner portion of the rear fuselage section with Model Master Gunmetal.

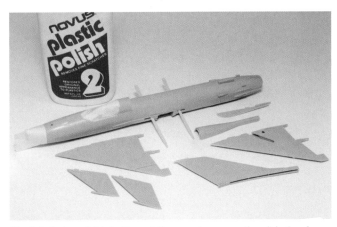

Fig. 11-4. A glossy finish for the metalizers requires a smooth, polished surface to work on. Buff these parts with Novus no. 2 plastic polish before airbrushing the metalizers onto the surfaces.

Step 3: The seat frame

Next is the seat frame. Mix a small amount of Tamiya Medium Gray, which usually requires a little thinner to flow properly. Add about 20 percent Tamiya thinner or rubbing alcohol to the paint, and test for flow.

When the flow is suitable, apply the paint with your airbrush. It should cover rapidly in several light coats. Once it's dry, you may also want to overcoat it with the Testors Dullcote Lacquer. Clean the airbrush thoroughly.

Step 4: Seat cushion and cockpit details

The seat cushion is painted in Tamiya Buff; again, thin the paint as described above and spray it through your fine/medium or general-purpose nozzle. Clean the airbrush thoroughly.

You will paint several small cockpit details in gunmetal shades. For this, use a bit of Testors Nonbuffing Gunmetal Metalizer. It requires no thinning and applies quickly with the same nozzle you've just used. Clean the airbrush with lacquer thinner afterwards.

Figure 11-1 shows the various components used in the cockpit assembly and forward section of the fuselage, with the paints used for each component. From this point, follow kit instructions to paint details and assemble the forward fuselage.

Step 5: The turbine engine

The rear section of the fuselage holds the turbine engine. This section is painted with Testors Gunmetal Buffing Metalizer. Paint each component of the engine with your airbrush. When the paint is dry, assemble the engine per kit instructions.

Paint the inner surfaces of the rear portion of the fuselage as well, and don't forget to clean the airbrush afterwards. When the paint is dry, assemble the fuselage per kit instructions.

Figure 11-3 shows the fuselage sections and the assembled turbine engine just prior to the assembly of the rear fuselage.

Step 6: Painting the fuselage

After assembling the main fuselage, you'll have to take a couple of steps to ensure a good finish. You'll want all the surfaces to appear extremely clean and polished to a shine.

The Metalizers spray on very thin and do not fill in any surface detail, so the surfaces to be painted must be filled and polished ahead of time. To give the "metal" surface a polished look, you must apply it over a glossy base.

After I filled all the seams on the fuselage, I polished them with polishing cloths and Novus no. 2 Plastic Polish (see fig. 11-4). After polishing, clean all surfaces with either rubbing alcohol or window cleaner to remove any trace amounts of polish or fingerprints, leaving a clean, glossy surface for the metalizers to adhere to.

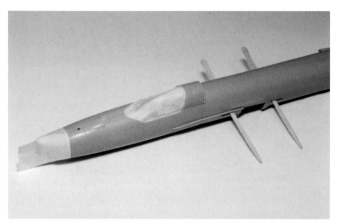

Fig. 11-5. After cleaning the buffed surfaces, mask off the completed cockpit and nosecone sections with drafting tape or Tamiya masking tape.

Fig. 11-6. The fuselage, after spraying and buffing with Model Master Aluminum Plate Metalizer. Notice the bright sheen that paint alone cannot provide.

The finished cockpit and nose must be masked; use a low-tack tape such as Scotch-brand Drafting Tape, or Tamiya masking tape (see fig. 11-5). Be careful to burnish the tape edges thoroughly, to prevent any of the airbrushed Metalizer paint from bleeding through onto the cockpit and nosecone.

After masking the cockpit and cleaning the fuselage, it's time to apply the main color to the aircraft. I used Testors Aluminum Plate Buffing Metalizer; as the most prominent color on the aircraft, it buffs to a nice sheen. Paint all portions of the aircraft this color as a basecoat. Apply the Metalizer with your medium or general-purpose nozzle, making sure to cover each surface thoroughly. The Metalizer goes on quickly, in very thin coats. Apply it directly from the jar, without thinner.

After painting all the parts, set them aside to dry, and clean the airbrush thoroughly with lacquer thinner. Figure 11-6 shows the fuselage painted in the Aluminum Plate Metalizer.

Step 7: Buffing and sealing

When the parts have dried, buff them to a sheen with a soft cloth like an old T-shirt or smooth rag, or a cotton swab. The finish will begin to shine. When you are satisfied with the result, you are ready to seal it.

Testors makes a Metalizer sealer, but later in this project, we will be applying an oil-based wash to the model. An oil wash would damage an enamel finish. Therefore, it is best at this point to apply Gunze Clear Acrylic as a sealer. Apply the clear with a general-purpose nozzle; thin it for smooth flow through your airbrush with Gunze thinner. Mix enough clear to cover the entire model and to use later as well.

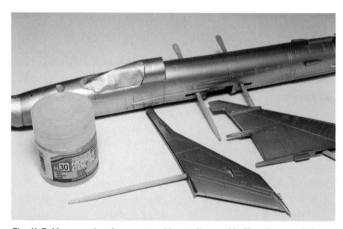

Fig. 11-7. After spraying these parts with metalizer and buffing them, seal them with Gunze Clear acrylic, which protects the finish and allows you to apply an oil wash to the surface without damaging it.

The clear applies very smoothly. Do not be alarmed that it dulls the polished finish under the clear slightly. It dries rapidly and shrinks down as it dries; therefore, it does not fill in or cover any details. The clear will protect further coats of Metalizers to be applied and protects the final finish from the oil wash.

After applying the clear acrylic, set it aside to dry thoroughly. Use a dehydrator if possible to accelerate the drying time. Clean the airbrush thoroughly, as you will be applying more Metalizer shades after this first clear coat.

Figure 11-7 shows various components that have been first sprayed with Aluminum Plate, buffed, and coated with Gunze Clear.

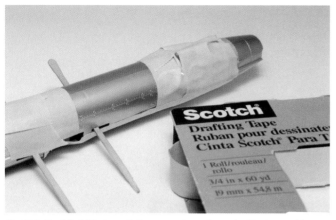

Fig. 11-8. Mask individual panels for contrasting colors using Tamiya masking tape or common drafting tape.

Fig. 11-9. Use Dark Anodonic Gray Metalizer for a darker metal shade on the fuselage.

Fig. 11-10. Buff the Dark Anodonic Gray Metalizer and coat it with Gunze Clear Acrylic, as you did with previous coats.

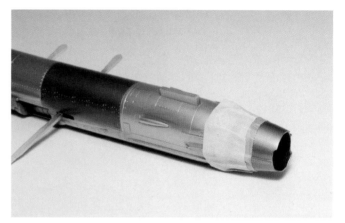

Fig. 11-11. The rear portion of the fuselage, masked with drafting tape, is ready to be painted in Gunmetal Metalizer, to match the previously painted inner portion and turbine.

Step 8: Additional metal shades

The next step is to begin masking and painting a variety of metal shades to the various components. Figure 11-8 shows the rear part of the fuselage masked with drafting tape. You'll paint this section with Dark Anodonic Gray Buffing Metalizer. After masking it, apply a few light coats of the Anodonic Gray to the fuselage (see fig. 11-9). Clean the airbrush again.

When it has dried, buff the Metalizer, and apply another coat of Gunze Clear over it. Clean the airbrush. After giving the clear a short time to dry, remove the masking tape (see fig. 11-10).

You will paint the rear portion of the fuselage a darker shade of Metalizer. When the clear has dried, mask the rearmost portion of the fuselage (see fig. 11-11). Spray the rear section in Gunmetal Buffing Metalizer (the color you used for the engine and inner portions of the rear fuselage section). Once it has dried, buff it and seal it with Gunze Clear, remembering to clean the airbrush after each session.

Paint the forward lip of the front fuselage the same color green as the nosecone. Figure 11-12 shows this section masked with a combination of Tamiya masking tape and drafting tape.

Fig. 11-12. Mask the fuselage lip around the nosecone and spray it with a bit of Gunze Clear (to prevent bleed-through). Then paint the lip in Radome/Hub Green to match the nosecone.

Seal the tape line with a light coat of Gunze Clear, and then cover the lip and nosecone with a coat of the Radome/Hub Green. Clean the airbrush.

When the paint is dry, remove the masking tape. Figure 11-13 shows the finished nosecone and lip.

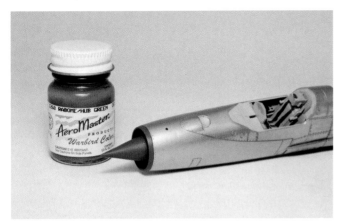

Fig, 11-13. Remove the masks from the finished nosecone and cockpit areas. Notice the clean paint separation lines.

Fig. 11-14. Mask various wing flaps for a contrasting coat of Stainless Steel Metalizer.

Fig. 11-15. These wings show the contrasting effect of adding Stainless Steel Metalizer to the previously painted Aluminum sections. Then buff all the sections and coat them with Gunze Clear for protection.

Fig. 11-16. You'll paint various sections in Nonbuffing Aluminum. Mask them, spray them with the metalizer, and seal them again with Gunze Clear Acrylic.

Fig. 11-17. The various metal shades in front of their respective paint bottles. The parts appear quite detailed at this point.

Fig. 11-18. Here you see Gunze Dark Green and Gray acrylic colors on the fuselage. Apply these as you did the metalizers and coat with Gunze Clear as well.

You will paint various surfaces of the wings and flaps in Stainless Steel Buffing Metalizer. Carefully mask these sections (see fig. 11-14), and apply the Metalizer. Clean the airbrush, buff the Metalizer, and cover these sections with Gunze Clear (see fig. 11-15).

Next, you will finish the top edge of the vertical stabilizer and a few sections of other components in a slightly different shade of aluminum—Nonbuffing Aluminum Plate, to give a different sheen than the Buffing variety. Mask the appropriate parts with drafting or fine-line tape (see fig. 11-16). Apply the Aluminum Nonbuffing Metalizer to these parts in a light coat; and once they're dry, seal them with Gunze Clear. Be sure to clean the airbrush after each step.

Figure 11-17 shows the various Metalizer shades on the vertical stabilizer and other components. The shades are very realistic and really make the parts look like they are made from metal, not painted plastic. Figure 11-18 shows the underside of the fuselage, with Gunze Dark Green and Gray colors added for detail

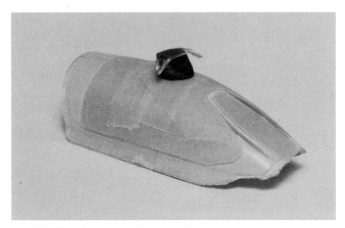

Fig. 11-19. Mask the canopy before painting it.

Fig. 11-20. Finish the landing gear and canopy parts in Aluminum Nonbuffing Metalizer.

as well (using the same steps as for all the other color panels).

The cockpit canopy is molded in clear, and is also to be painted in Aluminum Nonbuffing Metalizer. Mask it thoroughly (see fig. 11-19). Then apply a bit of Gunze clear to seal the edges, clean the airbrush, and add a coat of the Aluminum Metalizer. Figure 11-20 shows the finished canopy and a couple of landing gear parts also painted in Nonbuffing Metalizer. You can now paint-detail the canopy itself by hand and install it onto the aircraft.

Step 9: An oil-based wash

This kit is molded with an incredible array of engraved details, such as panel lines and rivets. These parts are easy to detail with an oil wash (see fig. 11-21). Mix the wash using your favorite shades of oil or enamel paints. Mix them with enough mineral spirits that they flow nicely into the engraved lines. Because you use an oil-based wash, it will not dry too rapidly. You'll be able to remove it with a paper towel and rag for a short time after applying it.

This also is a great way to weather the surface, as the wash dulls down the shiny surface of the clear underneath it, giving

Fig. 11-21. Here's the reason for the Gunze Clear coat. You can bring out all the fine engraved details–and get a bit of weathering–by adding an oil-based wash. Thin artist's oil paints with mineral spirits, and apply it with a soft, wide brush.

the model a very realistic, weathered appearance. With a little practice, it adds a nice level of detail to the model. You may also use materials such as SnJ aluminum polishing powder and powdered pastels to further bring out details on the model.

Fig. 11-22. Paint the rockets in Boyd White Primer.

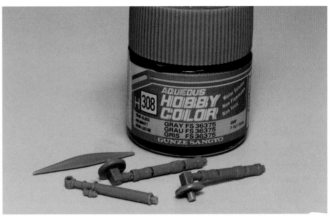

Fig. 11-23. Spray landing gear and other components with Gunze Gray acrylic.

Step 10: Small parts

Paint small parts, such as the rockets (see fig. 11-22), using Boyd White Primer. Mix this about 50:50 with thinner, apply to the rockets, and let dry. Clean the airbrush thoroughly. Paint the landing gear and various other components a light gray (see fig. 11-23). Paint these parts together, and let dry. Paint the tires and the instrument hood flat black; I used Tamiya Flat Black (see fig. 11-24).

Step 11: Assembling

After you airbrush all the parts, it's time to assemble the model and add any other brush-painted details. Follow the kit instructions closely, and try to save time by painting all the parts in a particular color at one time.

Add kit decals, and you're finished!

Fig. 11-24. Spray tires and instrument hood in Tamiya Flat Black acrylic.

The finished model, showing off the paint details that give it a very realistic appearance. Not bad for a first-time effort—from someone who has never built a jet before, much less one in raw-metal shades!

It's very realistic

The finished model turned out very realistic indeed. It compares well with photographs of real aircraft. With a combination of kit instructions and research materials, you can replicate even the most complicated paint finishes with ease.

The resulting finishes are much more realistic when you use your airbrush to apply the paint as thin and smooth as possible.

If you have a nearby air museum, it's a great place to familiarize yourself with the look of these aircraft—an opportunity to take notes and photographs to help you replicate these and other finishes for your models.

12

Camouflaged MiG

An Intricate but Simple-to-Apply Paint Scheme Brings This MiG 21 to Life

Aircraft models present a unique opportunity to try your talents at more than one style of airbrushing techniques. The MiG 21—the subject of this and the previous chapter—can be decorated not only in raw metal shades, but in several types of camouflage as well.

This project variation replicates an Indian Air Force MiG-21FL Type 77 paint scheme. If you have an airbrush with a fine detailing nozzle, you can duplicate the fine tiger-stripe camouflage theme on this aircraft very nicely.

This model was painted by Bob Holfels, using a Rich AB 200 airbrush. It is possible to replicate the pattern with other nozzles, but you'll have more control over your spray pattern using an airbrush with a fine-line nozzle. The Rich airbrush made it easy to paint the stripes.

The only caveat is that it is time-consuming, and you'll probably want to paint the stripes in one sitting. Make sure you have several hours of time, and you will enjoy the process.

Supplies needed

Model Master Pale Green
Gunze Sangyo FS 34092 Dark Green
Gunze Sangyo Clear Gloss

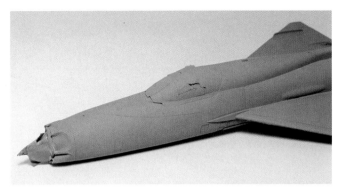

Fig. 12-1. After you paint and install the interior, nosecone, and engine and assemble the fuselage, then mask the fuselage and coat the model overall in Model Master Pale Green.

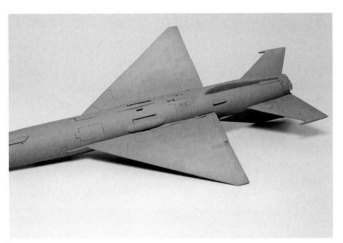

Fig. 12-2. Paint the undersides in metalizers (similar to the previous project, the all-metal version). Then mask these sections, as shown here, before painting the model pale green.

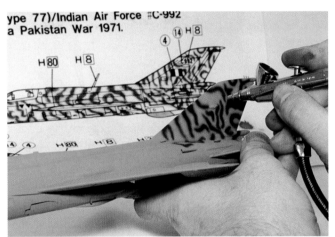

Fig. 12-3. Replicate the striped panels by spraying properly thinned Gunze Dark Green through a fine-detail airbrush over the Pale Green, using photocopied instructions and art as reference.

Step 1: Getting started

First: build, paint, and install the interior, nosecone, and engine into the fuselage, and attach the fuselage spine, vertical stabilizer, horizontal stabilizers, and wings per kit instructions. A little finish work is required to fill the leading edges of the wings and the vertical stabilizer.

After assembling these parts, carefully mask the cockpit, undersides of wings, and nosecone (see figs. 12-1 to 12-2). The undersides of the wings will be painted raw metal colors, similar to the MiG 21 project of the previous chapter.

Begin painting with a medium- to high-flow nozzle setup on your airbrush for good coverage. Mix the Model Master Pale Green to a milky consistency and test the flow and spray pattern before painting the body. Apply a general coat of the green, starting lightly and working up to a heavier flow that will quickly cover the base plastic. Once the body is fully covered, clean the airbrush thoroughly and let the model dry at least overnight (see fig. 12-1).

Step 2: Camouflage fine lines

The camouflage pattern is next, and is replicated using photocopies enlarged to the exact size of the model. Mix the Gunze dark green paint with thinner, and test the pattern on some scrap material. Carefully begin to "draw" the pattern onto the model, using the airbrush as if it were a drawing or writing instrument. Hold the airbrush very close to the model, generally less than one inch away, carefully controlling both spray pressure and paint flow. Hold the nozzle perpendicular to the surface; this is especially important with a fine pattern, as you want to avoid overspray as much as possible.

Practice this technique carefully until you are comfortable with the spray characteristics of the airbrush. This may sound more difficult than it actually is. The camouflage paint process is relatively easy but time-consuming. Carefully follow the photocopied patterns, and as you grow comfortable with the airbrush, the pattern will become easier to apply.

Figure 12-3 shows the application of the camouflage pattern copied from the instructions onto the vertical stabilizer.

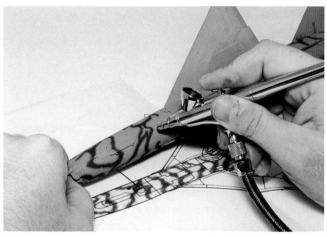

Fig. 12-4. "Draw" the camouflage directly onto the model at close range. First outline the large areas, as shown, and then fill them in with color. This will give you the best control of the camouflage shapes.

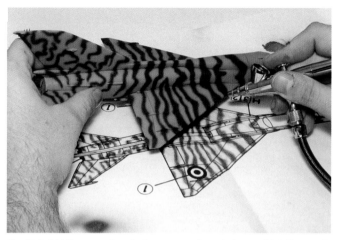

Fig. 12-5. Add the camouflage to the upper surfaces, being careful to line up all vertical and horizontal surfaces of the pattern.

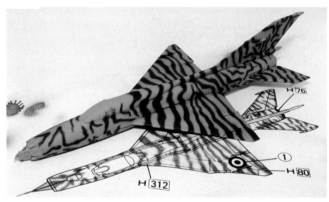

Fig. 12-6. The finished camouflage pattern matches the artwork quite nicely.

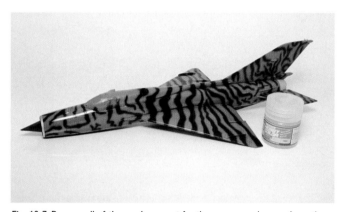

Fig. 12-7. Remove all of the masks except for the canopy, and cover the entire model in Gunze Clear Acrylic.

Step 3: Camouflage areas

Figure 12-4 shows the easiest way to replicate wider areas of camouflage. Spray the shape by first drawing the camouflage border with the airbrush, then fill in the section. This technique also helps to contain overspray. Figure 12-5 shows the application of the camouflage pattern to the wings and fuselage.

Figure 12-6 shows the finished camouflage job. After completing the dark green stripes, clean the airbrush thoroughly, and let the model dry.

Step 4: A clear coat

The next step is to remove the masking from the nosecone and wing undersides, leaving the cockpit mask in place. It's time to add a coat of Gunze Sangyo or a similar clear gloss acrylic to the model (see fig. 12-7).

Apply the clear paint with a medium- to high-flow nozzle, being careful not to add too much paint at once, which might fill in fine detail. Start with a fine mist, and progress to a heavier finish coat. Clean the airbrush thoroughly, and let the model dry before starting any further detailing.

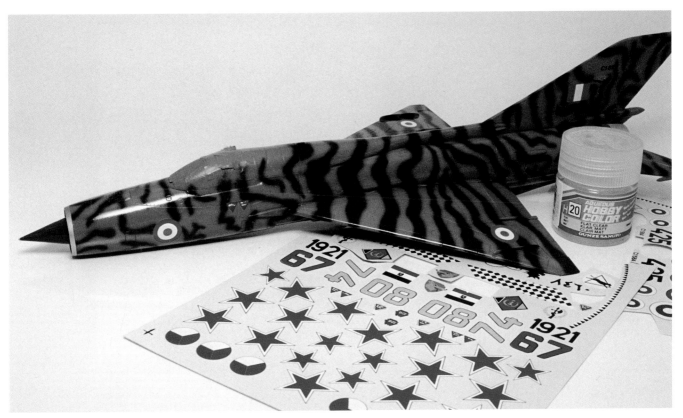

Fig. 12-8. The clear coat allows you to position the decals properly onto the model, without the silvering that would occur if you applied the decals over a flat finish.

Fig. 12-9. Apply an oil wash to bring out the finely engraved details and give the entire model a slightly weathered finish.

Fig. 12-10. Here you see the model with the various paints and materials used to achieve the finish. All that is left is to add a layer of AeroMaster or similar flat clear acrylic to tone down the glossy finish of the Gunze clear and the decals themselves.

Step 5: Decals and an oil wash

The next step is to add the decals to the model, letting them dry thoroughly (see fig. 12-8). Once they're dry, you can mix your artist's oils and mineral spirits for a wash (fig. 12-9 shows the wash materials you'll use). This wash will bring out engraved details such as panel lines and rivets. Wipe off any excess; this is easy to do because the clearcoat protects the finish from the wash.

After adding the wash, when you are satisfied with the results, seal the decals and oil-wash details with a general coat of flat clear (see fig. 12-10). Apply the clear with a medium- or high-flow nozzle, until you achieve a uniform, dull appearance. This coat will dry quickly; you will see the surface change from a wet gloss to a dull sheen shortly after you apply the clear. Clean the airbrush, and set the model aside to dry. It is now ready for finishing details, per kit instructions.

Fig. 12-11. The finished model is impressive indeed. It also shows how different the same basic model is from the raw metal finished one.

A model that stands out

This is a fun exercise that results in a stunning model (see fig. 12-11), quite different from the previous version of the MiG 21 in Chapter 11, finished in raw metal shades. This style of camouflage really stands out in a crowd, and thanks to a great tool like the fine-tip airbrush, it's easy to do.

With a bit of imagination, you could try this type of striped pattern on other models, like a safari vehicle.

Modeler Pat Covert built and super-detailed this "ready-to-rumble" engine. He achieved the metallic colors seen on this Ford Thunderbolt engine by using various Metalizer shades.

This customized VW Baja Beetle by Tamiya features a paint finish achieved in several steps. I first "primed" the body in Testors Sublime enamel, then covered it with a few coats of Colors by Boyd Bright Green Pearl, and finished with several coats of clear. The fenders are painted in Tamiya Neutral Gray mixed with a touch of green, then sprayed with an unthinned semigloss-clear mixture, giving the plastic parts the appearance of a pebble-grain. I painted the interior a combination of Neutral Gray and Sublime. Finally, I applied the seat pattern decals over the Sublime panels, and gave the interior a coat of Testors Dullcote Lacquer to achieve a flat sheen on all the parts, including the seat decals.

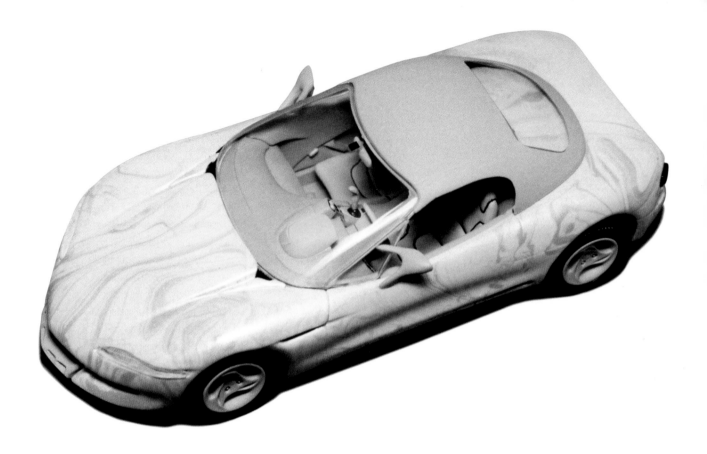

Above: Pat Covert built this swirl 'n pearl Stingray III. He applied the colorful paint job in a three-step layering process, starting with a white base coat. Then he sprayed several colors of paint onto the surface of water in a tub and immersed the model in that. By pulling the white body through the water and the fresh paint on the surface, he achieved the swirl effect on the body. He then airbrushed a light coat of pearl white paint over the swirl pattern.

Right: I painted this Corvette Spyder in PPG Harlequin paint. This paint changes colors, in this case from blue to red, when viewed at different angles. This amazing paint is extremely easy to apply. I first covered the body in black lacquer primer, then mixed a small amount of the PPG paint with PPG thinner and lightly misted it on the body in a few coats. The resulting color appears dull; it must be followed with a clear coat for the colors to take full effect.

Above: I painted this Plymouth Prowler snap-kit in a two-tone retro shade: turquoise over white (Gunze acrylics). I then clear-coated them with a blue-green flip-flop pearl mixed with the Gunze Clear Gloss. The interior colors match the exterior, covered in Testors Dullcote to replicate a leather sheen.

Right and below: I painted this Mercedes S 600 in Testors enamels to match the factory color. The body features a multicoat basecoat/clearcoat paint job, finished using Micro Mesh polishing cloths and Novus No. 2 plastic polish. I overcoated the lower body cladding with a semigloss clear, for a lower gloss level.

The interior is painted in low-gloss acrylics to simulate leather, overcoated with a Dullcote-gloss mixture to give it a scale sheen. The model received the Best Paint/Finish award at the 1997 GSL International Model Car Championship (No. 16).

Michael Laxton of Simi Valley, California, won the award for best finish at TamiyaCom 2000 for his work on this luscious red Porsche 911 made by Tamiya. Photo by Chris Appoldt

Far left: The Hulk is a vinyl kit built by Bob Holfels. He applied subtle shading and highlighting with an airbrush to give the model exceptionally fine surface depth and contrast. The result is a very realistic appearance.

Left: This 1/35 scale Steyr Kommandeurwagen kit made by Tamiya features a finely-drawn camouflage paint job by Robert Oehler. Photo by Chris Appoldt

Below: This 1/48 scale F-84G fighter was built and painted by modeler Daniel Clover, using Testors Buffable Metalizers. Photo by Chris Appoldt

Suppliers

Badger Air-Brush Co.
9128 W. Belmont Ave.
Franklin Park, IL 60131
800-247-2787

Binks Manufacturing
9201 W. Belmont Ave.
Franklin Park, IL 60131
847-671-3000

Paasche Airbrush Co.
7440 W. Lawrence Ave.
Harwood Heights, IL 60656-3497
708-867-9191

Tamiya
2 Orion
Aliso Viejo, CA 92656-4200
800-826-4922

Testor Corp./Aztek
620 Buckbee St.
Rockford, IL 61104-4891
815-962-7401

W. R. Brown Co.
901 E. Martin Luther King Jr. Dr.
North Chicago, IL 60064
800-662-3097

Automist 2000 Compressor, Rich AB 200 Airbrush and
other accessories are available from:
A1 Hobby Tools
Box 1496
Rockwall, Texas 75087
972-771-4588
www.automist2000.com

Pearl powders are available from:
Black Gold
2247 E. Division St.
Arlington, TX 76011

Paint supplies are available from:
MCW Automotive Finishes
P.O. Box 0518
Burlington, NC 27216-0518

This Demag D7 halftrack kit by Italeri
was built and painted by John Plzak
for the "Workbench Reviews" column
which appears monthly in *FineScale
Modeler* magazine. It features a
camouflage paint job that uses Polly
Scale Panzer Olive and Panzer Red-
brown, over a base of Polly Scale
Middlestone. Kalmbach photo